Cambridge Elements

Elements in Digital Literary Studies
edited by
Katherine Bode
Australian National University
Adam Hammond
University of Toronto
Gabriel Hankins
Clemson University

NEW APPROACHES FOR DIGITAL LITERARY MAPPING

Chronotopic Cartography

Sally Bushell
Lancaster University

Rebecca Hutcheon
Lancaster University

Shaftesbury Road, Cambridge CB2 8EA, United Kingdom

One Liberty Plaza, 20th Floor, New York, NY 10006, USA

477 Williamstown Road, Port Melbourne, VIC 3207, Australia

314–321, 3rd Floor, Plot 3, Splendor Forum, Jasola District Centre, New Delhi – 110025, India

103 Penang Road, #05–06/07, Visioncrest Commercial, Singapore 238467

Cambridge University Press is part of Cambridge University Press & Assessment, a department of the University of Cambridge.

We share the University's mission to contribute to society through the pursuit of education, learning and research at the highest international levels of excellence.

www.cambridge.org
Information on this title: www.cambridge.org/9781009478731

DOI: 10.1017/9781009353632

© Sally Bushell and Rebecca Hutcheon 2025

This publication is in copyright. Subject to statutory exception and to the provisions of relevant collective licensing agreements, with the exception of the Creative Commons version the link for which is provided below, no reproduction of any part may take place without the written permission of Cambridge University Press & Assessment.

An online version of this work is published at doi.org/10.1017/9781009353632 under a Creative Commons Open Access license CC-BY-NC 4.0 which permits re-use, distribution and reproduction in any medium for non-commercial purposes providing appropriate credit to the original work is given and any changes made are indicated. To view a copy of this license visit https://creativecommons.org/licenses/by-nc/4.0

When citing this work, please include a reference to the DOI 10.1017/9781009353632

First published 2025

A catalogue record for this publication is available from the British Library

ISBN 978-1-009-47873-1 Hardback
ISBN 978-1-009-35361-8 Paperback
ISSN 2633-4399 (online)
ISSN 2633-4380 (print)

Additional resources for this publication at www.cambridge.org/Bushell

Cambridge University Press & Assessment has no responsibility for the persistence or accuracy of URLs for external or third-party internet websites referred to in this publication and does not guarantee that any content on such websites is, or will remain, accurate or appropriate.

New Approaches for Digital Literary Mapping

Chronotopic Cartography

Elements in Digital Literary Studies

DOI: 10.1017/9781009353632
First published online: January 2025

Sally Bushell
Lancaster University

Rebecca Hutcheon
Lancaster University

Author for correspondence: Sally Bushell, s.bushell@lancaster.ac.uk

Abstract: This Element reconsiders what the focus of digital literary mapping should be for English Literature, what digital tools should be employed, and to what interpretative ends. How can we harness the digital to find new ways of understanding spatial meaning in the Humanities? The Element elucidates the relationship between literature, geography, and cartography and the emergence of literary mapping, providing a critique of current digital methods and making the case for new approaches. It explores the potential of Mikhail Bakhtin's 'chronotope' as a way of structuring digital literary maps that provides a solution to the complexities of mapping time and space. It exemplifies the method by applying it first as one of two approaches to mapping the realist novel by way of Dickens, and then to the multiple states of J. M. Barrie's *Peter Pan*. This title is also available as Open Access on Cambridge Core.

Keywords: literary mapping, digital literary maps, Chronotopic Cartography, digital literary studies, Bakhtin

© Sally Bushell and Rebecca Hutcheon 2025

ISBNs: 9781009478731 (HB), 9781009353618 (PB), 9781009353632 (OC)
ISSNs: 2633-4399 (online), 2633-4380 (print)

Contents

1 Approaches to Digital Literary Mapping   1

2 Back to Bakhtin: Understanding and Applying a Chronotopic Method   36

3 Towards a Processual Mapping Method: Evolving Neverland   69

4 Conclusion   94

References   96

Note: An online appendix for this publication can be accessed at www.cambridge.org/Bushell

1 Approaches to Digital Literary Mapping

[I]mprecision should be shown as precisely as possible.
(Piatti et al., 2009: 185)

[R]esistance to cartography is itself possessed of a truth function.
(Eve, 2022: 104)

This Element reconsiders what the focus of digital literary mapping should be for a subject like English Literature, what digital tools should be employed and to what interpretative ends. How can we harness the digital to find new ways of understanding spatial meaning in the Humanities? This short study offers a new way forward that focusses on mapping literature not just in absolute ways (onto pre-existing maps of the world) but also by relative means, using topology. A chronotopic approach understands the inter-fused nature of time and space (the chronotope) to be a vital constituent of literary works that requires alternative mapping methods. We argue that the creation of 'literary topology' as a new means of visualising and interpreting fictional and poetic time-space is not merely a preferable option to standard forms of mapping, but is inherently more suited to the needs of the Humanities.

In Section 1, we provide an overview of core concerns and questions that relate specifically to the digital mapping of literary place and space in order to contextualise and position our chronotopic approach. The Digital and Spatial Humanities is a relatively new field that is still in the process of self-definition. In a special issue of *DH Quarterly* focussed on Literary Studies, Pressman and Swanstrom state that

> [t]he Digital Humanities should not be understood as a new insurgent group retaliating against an older order. Instead, the DH identifies an emergent perspective for seeing how traditional literary scholarship provides the means for asking and pursuing interpretative questions, both about digital culture but also about other, older, and non-digital objects of study. (2013: 6)

We fully agree with such a statement. At the heart of DH lies a productive tension between scientific tools and the uses to which those tools are put, as well as between the interpretative methods and aims of traditional Humanities subjects and the application of such tools (or not) to these aims.

Broadly speaking, for the Sciences, knowledge (and thus the methods and tools by which knowledge is sought) is understood to be absolute, objective, evidence-based, and empirical. In contrast, for the Humanities, knowledge and understanding are of a radically different order: experiential, open to interpretation, ambiguous, multiple, changing, and open-ended. The medium in which such knowledge is held, and through which it is communicated, is that of language, in relation to which absolute understanding is often not an achievable goal (particularly in the most linguistically complex forms, for example, poetry). We argue therefore that subjectivity is *necessarily* built into any Humanities approach, even a computational one, and forms part of the subject under investigation. Equally, the fact that many digital projects are also essentially textual means that Humanities-based skills can come to the fore, if permitted.

While DH tools must remain necessarily 'scientific' to some degree (based upon mathematical and geometric models and algorithms), the uses to which they are put and the nature of the visualisations they produce do not have to be. Here Johanna Drucker's arguments are illuminating. Drucker makes a strong case for the need to reclaim visualisation tools for the Humanities:

> The majority of information graphics ... are shaped by the disciplines from which they have sprung: statistic, empirical sciences, and business. Can these graphic languages serve humanistic fields where interpretation, ambiguity, inference, and qualitative judgment take priority over quantitative statements and presentations of 'facts'? (2014: 5)

Focussed on the user interface, she sets out to 'consider how to serve a humanistic agenda by thinking about ways to visualize interpretation' (vii). Thus, she makes a core distinction between two *kinds* of visualisation:

> A basic distinction can be made between visualizations that are *representations* of information already known and those that are *knowledge generators* capable of creating new information through their use. ... Representations are static in relation to what they show and reference. ... Knowledge generators have a dynamic open-ended relation to what they can provoke. (65)

Such a distinction has particular resonance in relation to the approach we present here. Rather than thinking of map visualisations as absolute forms of knowledge presenting end results, we place focus on the act of generating maps so that the process is as important as the product, the maps are multiple, and the subjectivity of the critic as both reader and map-maker is taken into account.

This is important because it relates to another undeveloped aspect of working with literature digitally, noted by Martin Paul Eve. He makes the point that traditional literary criticism tends to elide its own process: 'what is usually of interest to those reading literary criticism is not the *process of how* the author arrived at the argument but the *outcome of the argument*' (Eve, 2022: 39). In contrast, Digital Literary Studies is more concerned with *how* conclusions are reached and even willing to narrate a negative return. From one point of view, this renders digital literary mapping more 'scientific', but from another it allows for new ways of 'doing' literary (and textual) criticism in the digital domain.

Having briefly outlined a larger need for DH tools and methods to be designed and shaped by the distinctive requirements of the Humanities, the rest of Section 1 looks at three key approaches currently dominant and of relevance to the specific field of digital literary mapping. These are the use of GIS tools when mapping literature onto geographic maps, the interdisciplinary concept of deep mapping as an alternative possible model, and the need for a hybrid methods/multi-scalar approach. Finally, we introduce 'literary topology' and explore the inherent subjectivity within chronotopic mapping as a positive.

Digital Literary Mapping and GIS: The Problem of Correspondence

There has long been a fascination with the relationship between literature and place: 'an impulse to map, to geovisualize the geographies of literature' (Mitchell, 2017: 85), but this has only fully come to fruition in the last ten years with the advent of new tools for digital mapping and visualisation. As a field, digital literary mapping emerges out of a prior subdiscipline within Literary Studies. The concept of Literary Geography originated in the late nineteenth and early twentieth centuries. Its starting point was authorial and concerned with literary touristic interest in place ('Brontë Country'; 'Dickens' London'), which developed by the mid-century into the popular concept of the Literary Atlas. The mapping of authors and texts illustratively *onto* place in such forms then spawned a far more conceptually advanced mode of literary mapping in the 1990s (led by Franco Moretti) – and out of this came digital literary mapping in the early twenty-first century.

Scholars such as Murrieta-Flores and Martin (2019) note that different disciplines have engaged with DH at different points in time: fields such as Archaeology made use of digital and spatial tools much earlier than others. One reason for delayed engagement in Literary Studies was the nature of the tools themselves, particularly in their first iteration as complex GIS technologies such as ArcGIS.

In *Abstract Machine*, Charles Travis opens with the cave paintings of the Lascaux Caves as an example of 'primal GIS' (2015: 4), reminding us that the term 'Geographic Information System' can be applied to any form of spatial visualisation. In our own time, however, GIS relates specifically to digital software that allows for the visual presentation of geographic information in a range of readable ways. Travis gives a useful technical summary:

> A geographic information system, or GIS, provides a digital platform upon which multiple map layers (called *shapefiles* and *rasters*) electronically stack

on top of each other to create composite images. Each shapefile layer and its attendant data table display unique variables (represented as points, polylines, and polygons). Layers can also be composed of a pixelated terrain or map images called rasters. (2015: 5)

In its standard iteration, then, GIS technology draws upon Cartesian and Euclidean geometry and is quantitative in nature – gathering and analysing numerical data and projecting this onto a co-ordinate grid system. Such a model still contains subjective input even when automated (in terms of data selection, correction of computer error in geoparsing, and so on), but the dominant impulse is towards minimising subjectivity. Of course, standard GIS tools *can* be adapted to more qualitative uses – indeed, the combining of the quantitative and qualitative is a vibrant area of DH.[1] Still, inherent positivism remains at odds with the more metaphysical needs of the Humanities. As Taylor and Gregory put it:

GIS's major strength is also its fundamental weakness: the highly quantitative structure that allows us to undertake spatial analysis also depends on translating complex, ambiguous sources into more definite numerical data (such as specific coordinates). This approach also risks stripping the map of its affective meaning. (2022: 49)

One effect of this is that GIS methods applied to powerful, even traumatic, experiences can have unforeseen consequences. In exploring the representation of the Holocaust as a geographic as well as historical event, Cole and Hahmann note:

Troublingly, GIS tools have so far proven better suited to working with the documents produced by the perpetrators with their chimera of certainty ... than the post-war testimony of Holocaust survivors ... [A]dopting GIS tools has tended to privilege understandings of perpetrator space over victim experiences of genocidal place. (2019: 40)

In this highly-charged example, the need for alternative approaches is strongly felt.

We can consider such issues further, as they impinge upon the mapping of literary place and space, by looking at two attempts to use GIS for digital literary mapping and at some of the problems that rapidly emerge. The first major digital literary mapping project – *A Literary Atlas of Europe* (2006–) – took its impulse from the paradigm shift initiated by Franco Moretti when he redefined literary maps, 'not as metaphors, and even less as ornaments of discourse, but as analytical tools that dissect the text ... bringing to light relations that would otherwise remain

---

[1] See the papers in the special section of *IJHAC* edited by John Stell on combining qualitative and quantitative approaches: *International Journal of Humanities and Arts Computing* 13.1–2 (2019).

hidden' (Moretti, 1998: 4). For this project, cartographers and literary scholars worked together to create a prototype quantitative mapping model for literature with the potential to be rolled out at a large scale (Piatti et al., 2009). The digital *Atlas* focussed on three test areas (a lake, a coastal region, a city) with five fictional elements mapped across texts and authors to create a spatial database capable of generating automated maps. The core geometric elements were 'setting'; 'projected space'; 'route'; 'waypoint'; and 'marker'. The model attempted to allow for non-place-specific spatial elements in fiction ('projected space') as well as for differing degrees of distance from the geographic.[2]

Right from the start, the *Literary Atlas* identified that 'the geography of fiction must be characterised as a rather uncertain or imprecise geography' (Reuschel et al., 2009: 6) and stated:

> Fictional spaces are artificially created by description in prose by the author. They do not have definite borders, are often hard to localize and shift on a scale between strong and weak relation to the actual geospace. (1)

To allow for this, in visualising 'setting', the problem of indeterminacy was presented through colour fading and fuzzy images. For 'routes', equally, the multiplicity of options left implicit in a text led the project to create three categories: 'taken from the text'; 'plausible'; and 'interpreted' (9). Thus, the *Literary Atlas* rapidly identified a number of unique attributes of literary place and space that were revealed by the challenges of attempting to map it onto the physical world – that is to say, the *resistance* of literary place to being fixed, not least because 'a specific feature of a literary space is its numerous gaps' (Piatti et al., 2009: 185).

At the same time, a comment such as the one quoted in the previous paragraph concerning fictional spaces makes clear the way in which the project was weighted towards the geographic. A literary scholar would never describe fictional spaces as 'artificial' and such a comment is in danger of falling into the 'referential fallacy' – mistaking the map for the territory, the word for the thing, and failing to understand that the 'real' does not lie behind the fictional, or constitute its ground.[3] As a result, a major weakness of the project is that it is constantly centred on a desire to be 'accurate' and to fix correspondence in a way that is problematic and near-paradoxical:

> It is mandatory to determine the identity of the setting: textimmanent names (*direct referencing*) or names deduced indirectly from other sources or

---

[2] The most detailed account of the maps in action is given in Piatti et al., 2011.
[3] Counter to this, Piatti does allow for 'faint and strong correspondences between geospace and textual space' and notes 'both writers and readers are tempted by the option of anchoring texts somehow in the real world' (2009: 182).

researches (*indirect referencing*). For example in Thomas Mann's famous novel 'Buddenbrooks' (1901), Lübeck as the main setting is never named. Yet through a couple of hints (Travemünde and the Baltic Sea are mentioned), it becomes evident, that no other town can be filled in. At the same time the level of accuracy has to be estimated. (Reuschel et al., 2009: 3)

Here we feel the danger of strongly privileging the known *over* the represented or imagined – which the act of correspondence to actual sites in the world encourages.

Many of the challenges experienced by the project team can be seen to be created by the nature of the GIS tools being used and their implicit imperatives. What the resistance to representation really tells us is that these tools do not allow Humanists to do what they want, or need, to do with the relationship between literary place and space and real-world geography. In a chapter on 'Maps and Place' in *The Digital Humanities and Literary Studies* Martin Paul Eve sums this up well:

> [D]igital mapping approaches demonstrate to us the problems in transposing literary texts, which use their space as narrative structuration devices, onto maps that purport to represent an extra-textual reality. Like all good humanistic inquiry, digital mapping does not simply produce positivistic answers to scientifically framed questions. Because the two – maps and reality, or mapping questions and cartographic answers – do not piece together neatly like a jigsaw. They rather sit in a relationship of mutual tension and productive questioning. (Eve, 2022: 178)

Let's turn to a second example of relatively early adaptation of GIS software for the mapping of literature: Charles Travis's attempt to map Homer and Dante onto the map used by James Joyce for *Ulysses*.[4] Travis provides a solid authorial rationale, based on Joyce's famous comment that he aimed to 'give a picture of Dublin so complete that if the city one day suddenly disappeared from the earth it could be reconstructed out of my book' (Budgen, 1972: 69) and on the fact that Joyce wrote *Ulysses* in Paris using a 1904 map of Dublin.

Travis employs the 1904 map as the base layer and argues for a writerly process that combines detailed map knowledge with the development of intersecting narratives:

> Joyce used *Thom's* directory and map to erect Cartesian scaffolding over the city of Dublin. In this framework, and influenced by Classical Greek and Medieval Italian epic poetry, he stitched together the book's plotlines. Once he had sewn the fabric of his book together, Joyce dismantled the cartographic structure. (Travis, 2015: 63)

---

[4] Travis does this first in Chapter 5 of *Abstract Machine* (2015), then returns to it in 'Joycean Chronotopography' (2017).

In this example of digital literary mapping, then, the tools are used in two ways: to reconstruct an earlier stage of (cartographic) authorial creative process, and to integrate this visually with other spatial forms from influential intertexts.

Travis's approach is sophisticated and ambitious. It is informed by Deleuzian theory as well as biographical and contextual knowledge about writerly process and seeks to advance *three* different forms of 'interpretive visualisation' at the same time: 'hermeneutic (textual and topological), ergodic (mapping alternative narrative paths in a "cybertext"), and deformative (deliberate textual misreadings)' (Travis, 2015: 64). The total version of Dublin, Homer, and Dante combines the verticality of Dante's layers with the routes of characters across the city and Odyssean journeys (see Figure 1) – these maps are also given in much greater detail as a separate series. Thus, although Travis uses some standard GIS tools, he also combines these with a layered approach that visualises entirely fictional spatial movement. The aims of the visualisation are also therefore multiple:

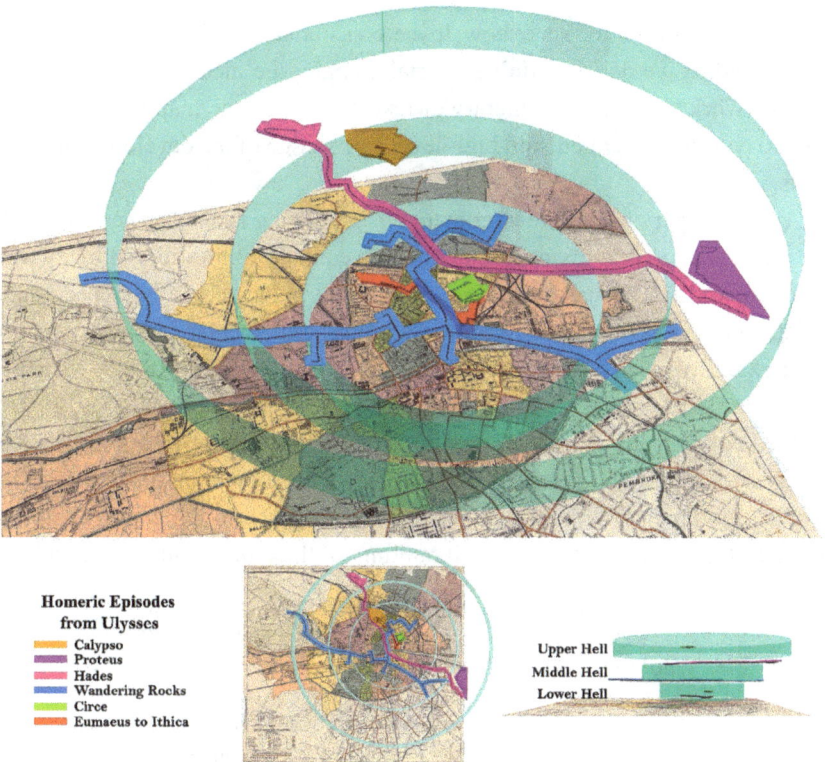

Figure 1 Charles Travis: Arcscene visualisation of Ulysses in *Abstract Machine*, 79. Reproduced by kind permission of the author.

> This GIS model serves three objectives. The first seeks to create a topographical picture of Dublin using the cartographical source material that Joyce used to plot his novel. The second translates Joyce's 'cut-and-paste' and other visual and literary methods into GIS form. The third explores and maps how Joyce narratively and topologically linked various Dublin locations to selected Homeric episodes with symbolic references to Dante's journey. (Travis, 2015: 64)

Finally, Travis also makes the crucial point that the visualisations are part of a process rather than an authoritative single map.

There is much to admire in the creativity and ambition shown here, but also plenty to critique. For example, locating the authority of the intersecting map visualisations for Homer and Dante authorially in Joyce is problematic since it necessarily moves into speculation:

> ArcMap and ArcScene helped to create a 3D model that overlaid Homer's and Dante's schemas and topologies onto a digitized *Thom's* map of Dublin to visualize how Joyce conceptualized the voyages of Bloom and Dedalus. (2015: 77)

Do we really know for sure 'how Joyce conceptualized' his characters' journeys? And, if we do, shouldn't authorial mapping be incorporated explicitly? For the work to convince a literary or textual scholar, the mapping of process should be fully integrated with high-level knowledge of the development of the texts.

A fuller experience of the intertextual interweaving is also needed alongside the visualisations of individual routes (which equate Dublin streets directly with layers in Hell and stages of Odysseus's journey). This could have been done using digital tools (combining GIS with corpus linguistics) to map and visualise intertextuality much more directly, but also to think about how best to visualise the intertextual space itself. Equally, for the project to be rigorous, if it is concerned with Joyce's process one might want the base text to be that of draft materials rather than the published text, for each section of the map. This would also potentially introduce a more dynamic spatio-temporality into the visualisation in terms of the gradual building of the modern odyssey across the different spaces of the city.

In their recent book, Taylor and Gregory outline three phases for Digital Humanities scholarship and argue that we are moving into the third of these:

> In the first, databases, corpora, and/or techniques are developed to explore the potential of digital methods in advancing knowledge about a particular kind of source. In the second, method or data-led research starts to be conducted using these new resources, with the aim of exploring, explaining and

critiquing these new opportunities. A third stage involves moving the humanities back into the foreground by using the technology to develop nuanced responses to applied research questions on topics that are derived primarily from the sources rather than the technology. (2022: 52)

When we compare the work of the *Literary Atlas of Europe* project with Travis's mapping of *Ulysses*, the rapid advances made in the use of GIS tools seem to enact the move from phases one and two to three (and do so in less than a decade).

Digital Deep Mapping

An alternative approach to the limitations of standard GIS mapping that is often cited (and could be envisaged for Travis's work with Joyce) is that of the 'deep map'. This position emerges as resistance to, or an adaptation of, GIS methods and tools to more creative ways of engaging with place and space. However, deep mapping is a difficult approach to pin down.[5] It locates its own pre-digital origins in a detailed multimedia presentation of place (*PrairyErth*) that combined travel writing with interviews, local myths, factual information, and cartography.[6] Thus, it is a method of mapping with a strong underlying ethos: a desire to tell stories about place, or present place through multiple forms in an inclusive way. Although not originally created for the digital domain, it lends itself to digital mapping because of its inherent cross-generic, interdisciplinary, and multimedia tendencies.

The implication of this for digital tools and methods is perhaps most clearly understood in comparison with traditional cartography. Deep mapping explicitly differentiates itself from both 2D map representations and Cartesian principles, in which 'an emphasis on absolute space based on Euclidean coordinate systems often frustrates the humanist's effort to understand how spaces change over time and how spatial relativities emerge and develop' (Bodenhamer et al., 2013: 174). In the discipline of History, where deep mapping has so far found greatest traction, it 'embraces multiplicity, simultaneity, complexity and subjectivity' and advocates a far more 'bottom up' approach: 'In it we do not find the grand narrative but rather a spatially facilitated understanding of society and culture embodied by a fragmented, provisional, and contingent argument with multiple voices and multiple stories' (Bodenhamer et al., 2017: 5).

---

[5] For a useful attempt to do so, see Clifford McLucas: 'The Ten Tenets of Deep Mapping', https://cliffordmclucas.info/deep-mapping.html.
[6] See Moon, 1991.

Deep mapping thus also suggests a particular approach towards its subject which is highly performative and has a 'processual underpinning' (Springett, 2015: 624). This lends itself particularly to visual and performance art, which may be the best medium for the concept:

> Deep maps go beyond description or simple communication, rather they are an *enaction* of place. They offer a certain type of storytelling that seeks to democratise knowledge, through the use of *the map*. (Springett, 2015: 624)

Thus, practitioners such as Ian Biggs develop a model of deep mapping as artistic practice focussed on the rich temporal processes in place that can also inform the work of art itself.[7]

Perhaps the best worked-through example of academic deep mapping to date is the Lancaster University project: *Geospatial Innovation in the Digital Humanities: A Deep Map of the Lake District* (2015–2018) and its resulting publications.[8] In *Deep Mapping the Literary Lake District: A Geographical Text Analysis*, Taylor and Gregory provide a convincing model that successfully combines 'quantitative methods with a detailed understanding of the historical, cultural and geographic contexts in which these texts were written' (2022: 23). Centred on a textual corpus of Lake District writing, chapters then work across nineteenth- and twenty-first-century concerns seeking to 'interpret the apparently objective data displayed in GIS through a subjective lens' (2022: 63). It should be noted, however, that although the *book* explores these concepts fully, there is no digital 'deep map' website produced as an exemplar. Equally, although it engages with the literary, the core textual focus is on travel writing rather than fiction so that the relationship between geographic maps and texts remains relatively unproblematised.

Cultural Geographer Les Roberts' consideration of deep mapping in terms of diachronic and synchronic relations also seems highly relevant here (Roberts, 2016).[9] If Archaeology deals (at least primarily) with physical, material layers of meaning, and History with an intermingling of the material and textual, Literary Studies is just as layered but has to handle a more problematic relationship to both geography and the map (as we have seen). A literary work also has multiple temporalities in play that are of equal importance. Diachronically, the work stands in relation to its own past production (acts and sites of writing, pre-text and draft materials) as well as future versions of itself (later revisions, republication in different contexts, etc.). Synchronically, it presents multiple moments of horizontal connection at points of contingent completion or publication that generate reader-reception and response beyond the control of the author.

---

[7] For example, see Bailey and Biggs, 2012.   [8] Bushell was a co-investigator on this project.
[9] See also Bushell, 2016: 137–41.

Representationally, the literary world generates its own place and space at different distances from the world according to literary form and with radically varying degrees of representation of external and inner space. Shelley Fisher Fiskin defines such maps as 'palimpsests in that they allow multiple versions of events, of texts, of phenomena (both primary and secondary) to be written over each other – with each version still visible under the layers' and one can envisage a rich and complex 'deep text' model for a digital edition working in such a way.[10] Thus, the potential for a highly complex structure of digital literary deep mapping is certainly present, but not yet developed.

With the advent of 'neogeography' or non-expert mapping (Mitchell, 2017) a set of new tools and methods for Web 2.0 have started to open up mapping to the general public, as well as to Humanities scholars not highly trained in computer programming. Geovisualisation tools release the user from the need to pinpoint a place to a specific location upon the earth's surface and allow for freer, more experimental, and more self-aware modes of mapping literature onto the historic, or for the combining of 2D and 3D models. Nonetheless, at the time of writing, deep mapping is more theorised than practised (beyond the field of art) and Literary Studies remains sceptical. Les Roberts goes so far as to suggest that deep mapping 'should be implicit not explicit in its application' (2016: 4). In a sense this returns us to our starting point: deep mapping's resistance to definition. Perhaps it is more about an underlying *stance* within the Spatial Humanities than it is a method in and of itself.

Quantitative versus Qualitative, Macro- versus Micro-Mapping

In their work on the geography of the Holocaust mentioned previously, Cole and Hahmann describe the experience of scale for those living through the event:

> Scale operates metaphorically as a set of Russian dolls (Herod 2010), with the body inside the local, inside the regional, inside the national, inside the continental, inside the global. Survivors tend to move in between these scales in narratives that are spatially (and oftentimes also temporally) dynamic rather than fixed. (2019: 41)

They suggest that such complex human experiences can only be visualised and mapped effectively by using a dynamic and multi-scalar mapping model. They conclude by making three crucial points concerning the value of relative mapping using a network model as opposed to the point-based specificity of GIS:

---

[10] Fishkin, 2011, https://escholarship.org/uc/item/92v100t0.

> Alongside the possibility of zooming in and out of the scales of narratives, the use of a graph representation allows for the inclusion of the varying degrees of certainty and uncertainty found within humanities sources in the database. ... But it is not simply the case that rethinking database design enables us to work with the complexity of the kind of narratives that digital humanists encounter. They also enable us to undertake new forms of analysis from this complex data. (Cole and Hahmann, 2019: 49)

All three of the points made here (the need to zoom in and out; the representation of uncertainty; the two-way learning process in adapting digital tools) are also of vital importance to the mapping of literary place and space. Visualisations need to be able to move between whole text, chapter, page, and paragraph level – as well as to allow for the different spatial experiences of multiple characters, narrators or narratives, and readers – and the spatial indeterminacies and dislocations built into these. Furthermore, the engagement between texts and tools needs to generate new forms of analysis extending easily out of the old. Apart from enriching the Digital and Spatial Humanities, this is also essential if such work is to become a fully integrated element of its core disciplines.

Such a call for macro- and micro-mapping intersects with the prior debate in Digital Literary Studies between 'distant' and 'close' reading – which crudely corresponds to 'zooming out' and 'zooming in'. In its first major phase (roughly 2005–20), DH focussed primarily on quantitative analysis as a consequence of its origins in Moretti's call for large-scale 'literary history' and his desire to open up Literary Studies to quantifiable methods. This emphasis was also logical, since it made the best case for the new insights offered by computational approaches (i.e. the computer's ability to read at scale will always exceed the capacities of a human reader). More recently, however, the distant/close reading debate has been accused of creating a false binary between past and present practices. Even so, that binary points to an underlying issue that is harder to dismiss: should Digital Literary Studies be concerned with respecting the uniqueness of the computational tools and thus privilege the new *medium* allowing it to reconfigure our understanding of the home discipline; or should the discipline be seeking to reshape digital tools and methods to enable integration of more familiar exploration of texts in known ways?

It is telling that, in order to make arguments that prioritise new ways of counting-as-reading *over* traditional hermeneutics ('close reading'), the works of literary criticism that are targeted for critique by DH scholars are more than sixty years old. So, Matthew Jockers in *Macroanalysis* takes issue with Erich Auerbach's *Mimesis* (1946) and Ian Watt's *The Rise of the Novel* (1956), while Andrew Piper critiques a metonymic model at the heart of close reading, again using Auerbach (Jockers, 2013: 7; Piper, 2018: 7–8). Why is this? Primarily because the current discipline of Literary Studies in the twenty-first century is self-aware, wide-ranging, and highly interdisciplinary. Any *recent* work of literary criticism will undertake textual analysis in conjunction with cross-disciplinary theory and complex philosophical, social, and ideological ideas. Thus, the reduction of intellectual activity to close reading of the canon (necessary to assert the superiority of distant reading in comparison) can *only* occur by temporal displacement. To be fair to the discipline, Jockers and Piper should be choosing an influential literary-critical study published post-2000. They cannot do this, because then the evidence base for the 'before' to their 'after' would *not* be a narrow close reading of a few canonical texts.[11]

Another key issue in the attacks on close reading is the false presentation of it as if it were a *method* when it is in fact a *skill*. In contemporary literary criticism the ability to undertake high-level analysis of a text is simply one key attribute among many (e.g. Derrida was a great close reader, but this hardly defines him). This clarification is important, because it allows for a very different way of integrating DH with the core Humanities subjects, *without* the need to aggressively redetermine the source discipline. An approach that *combines* the quantitative and the qualitative should be able to function as another form of interdisciplinarity in which the reading of literary texts in one way and through one frame can be placed alongside the reading of texts in a different way, through another. Admittedly the medium itself is of a different order, but this just makes for a unique interdisciplinary relationship. Our own position therefore is to advocate a middle ground in which each side is open to the other (enlightened cross-fertilisation).

The field of Digital Literary Studies is in a process of recalibration, but the resistant position to distant reading still tends strongly towards identifying quantitative methods as *already present* within Literary Studies in order to justify this approach at macro- and micro-levels rather than integrating with traditional interpretative practices. In *Enumerations*, Piper explicitly wants to move on from 'overly binary models of reading largely untethered from past practices' (2018: x). But to do this, his study seeks to locate quantitative elements within the core discipline – identifying the 'building blocks of literary study' in terms of areas such as 'punctuation in poetry', 'emplotment in novels', and 'dispersion of topics' (3).

---

[11] The metonymic argument *does* still partly apply (a sample stands in for the whole) but this criticism would be true of any Humanities discipline since it relates to the human capacity for understanding. In any case, distant reading itself is also doing this, just at a larger scale. See Jin, 2017 and Piper, 2013 (where he also argues that topology is both metonymic and metaphorical).

For his part, Martin Paul Eve inverts the distant reading model by applying computational methods to a single text (David Mitchell's *Cloud Atlas*) focussing closely on linguistic patterns and shifts that are otherwise not obvious when reading. The analyses enabled by Eve's 'Computational Formalism' (Eve, 2019: 21) work 'through a type of deformative reconstruction, they make clear something that was directly under our noses but that still required elucidation' (19). However, the nature of this 'close reading' – of variants across published texts or genre identified through 'microtectonic linguistic shifts' and stylometry (22) – feels very different from the disciplinary norm. Eve's position – emphasising, on the one hand, that distant reading existed within Literary Studies long before computers, and, on the other, that close reading can be undertaken by a computer, not just a literary critic – thus makes the case for automation at macro- and micro-levels, but the nature of the 'close reading' is really just *distant reading on a small scale*. Thus, such approaches helpfully seek to make a bridge between the home discipline and DH, but *not* between qualitative and quantitative methods. Our position is different from these, since we do not feel the need to negate or redetermine long-standing interpretative activities in the home discipline at the expense of DH, but seek to combine the two – folding past methods into the present and future.

A multi-scalar model is another way of bridging between traditional Literary Studies and Digital Literary Studies and between verbal and visual needs. As English and Underwood make clear, in their introduction to a special issue on the subject, Literary Studies has always been in part 'a drama of competing scales' and close reading can itself be viewed as an example of 'scalar contraction' (2016: 278) which reached its peak in the 1970s before an opposing expansion into a 'crisis of largeness' (2016: 281). Jay Jin develops such ideas by drawing out the ways in which close/distant is also synecdoche/metonymy and makes the helpful point that perhaps the real threat of close reading is that 'closeness ... marked a synecdochic relationship that removed the need for scale altogether' (2017: 112). The DH relationship between macro and micro, or quantitative and qualitative, analysis has also tended to be sequential – from counting to reading, from information to interpretation – but this does not have to be the case. Jin's suggestion that '[I]nstead of complementarity or linear sequence, one can conceptualize a recursive relationship between "close" and "distant", a continual back-and-forth' (2017: 116) is one that we embrace: an iterative approach.

In an article concerned with macro-/micro-analysis for the Spatial Humanities specifically, Taylor et al. provide a detailed account of a 'multi-scalar' approach that works in such a way. Exploring soundscapes in the Lake District, the team first uses computational macro-analysis to identify texts from across the entire corpus, which particularly focus upon sound; then read these texts closely, before undertaking a second sweep for emerging concepts such as 'echo'. This circular structure allows for more traditional hermeneutic activities to be combined with computational (see also Bushell et al., 2022a, 2022b). An iterative approach forms the basis for the topological method as it is fully developed in relation to *fictional* place and space for the rest of this Element and lies at the heart of our method.

Literary Topology and Chronotopic Mapping

Topology releases the mapping of spatial meaning from the cartographic. It offers a simpler alternative to using a full GIS apparatus and generates a different *kind* of map. As we have seen, GIS is concerned with a Cartesian map model based upon accuracy to points on the world's surface. Topology is centred upon interconnections between the elements mapped, but not necessarily with their correspondence to anything else (though a topological map can still be layered onto the real, or combined with GIS). The topology *is* still a mathematical model, a generated algorithm (and it functions as an underlying element of complex GIS tools such as ArcGIS). But we can also adapt its use to non-scientific ends and use it to pursue interpretative questions in more visually accessible ways that are inherently more suited to the needs of the Humanities.

A topological model is one in which all elements within a contained totality are related to each other in a way that may change across the whole. Not only that, but it can be anchored to the real as needed, yet also move beyond it if place becomes internalised in memory, dreams, fantasy, dislocation, or distortion. The primary focus is on 'shape, connection, relative position compared with that of geometry (or geography) which are about more rigid notions such as distance angle and area' (Earl, 2019: 2–3). It is perhaps worth noting that this alternative approach for digital literary mapping was always implicitly present in Moretti's own early work where he observed that *'geometry "signifies" more than geography'* (2005: 56, italics original).[12]

In a rich paper on the potential of topology for literature, Piper argues that the forms of topology enabled by an electronic environment represent a paradigm shift in terms of the reader's relationship to language as 'a form of action rather than expression' so that 'topology encourages us to re-encounter, anew, the visuality of reading' in a way that 'alters our visual and cognitive relationship to the text' (Piper, 2013: 377). He concludes:

> Reading topologically is an entry into the knowledge of scale and knowledge as scale. Instead of the absolutes of distant or close, we should be thinking in terms of scalar reading. (382)

---

[12] John Stell also comments that 'this tension between topological and geometric information is evident in the maps and diagrams of Moretti' (2019: 24).

What is in play here is a part–whole relation that allows for an easy slippage across and between visual and verbal forms.

A topological approach emerges out of the adaptation of social network theory to Literary Studies. There have been various attempts to adapt the use of a graph network for literature over the last fifteen years but all prior efforts have been centred upon relationships between characters within a text, rather than seeking to map places and spaces in the narrative (as we do in the *Chronotopic Cartographies* project). Following Rydberg-Cox's work on Greek drama (2011), much of the research has been centred on different dynamics between character groupings within the whole (single central character; two factions; clusters; anomalies). While Rydberg-Cox's work uses the stage, and appearances on it by actors, to determine points of contact, the work of Elson, Dames, and McKeown is centred upon an attempt to 'derive the networks from dialogue interactions' and includes automated 'components for finding instances of quoted speech, attributing each quote to a character, and identifying certain characters who are in conversation' (Elson et al., 2010: 138). A similar model is explored by Moretti in his Stanford LitLab pamphlet 'Network Theory, Plot Analysis'. Here, Moretti draws a direct equivalence between *plot* and network – although plot is determined in terms of character rather than narrative: 'A network is made of vertices and edges; a plot of characters and actions: characters will be the vertices of the network, interactions the edges' (Moretti, 2011: 2).

In contrast to such pre-existing network models, our chronotopic method is centred upon *spatio-temporal meaning across the narrative* and thus allows greater space for the exploration of structure, narrative, event, and plot, as well as of spatiality (human lived experience) represented within this. A full account of the technical method is provided in the Online Methodological Appendix, but it can also be summarised briefly here, along with key tables.

A bespoke spatial schema for chronotopic mapping was developed by the team and applied manually to texts to enable graph generation out of them.[13] A text is marked up by chunking out sections in terms of both location and chronotopic identity and this generates the nodes of the graph topology. The identity of the chronotopes derives primarily from the account given by Russian theorist Mikhail Bakhtin ([1937], 1984) but with the necessary additions of 'distortion' and 'metanarrative' (see Table 1). Nodes are then connected to each other by different forms of connection allowing for direct, indirect, and internal movement (see Tables 2 and 3). Within a node, place names (toporefs) are also identified with varying levels of distance from representational place.

---

[13] James Butler was the linguist on the team, with primary responsibility for developing the schema.

Table 1 Chronotopic symbols and descriptions

Symbol	Name	Description
	Encounter	An unexpected happening, sudden shift, any meeting. Can occur anywhere, but frequently on the road.
	Road	Paths, travel, journey, options, coming and going, wandering.
	Castle	Confinement, imprisonment, stasis, discomfort, dark, visible traces of the past.
	Idyll	Familiarity, comfort, happiness, pleasure, peace, respite, self-contained, unified, stable, homely, known.
	Idyllic Wilderness	The wild, openness, freedom, untouched, the earth, the natural world, unity.
	Anti-Idyll	Dystopias, post-apocalyptic settings, mechanical, the idyll destroyed, invaded, or made alien. Can be exterior or interior.
	Threshold	The hall, the corridor, the staircase, the street, docks, stations, liminal spaces, emotionally charged, intense, sublime, excess, a place of contrasts.
	Parlour	Interior, room, defined, bounded, hosting guests, where the public and private merge, where dialogues happen, a site of political and commercial intrigue.
	Provincial Town	Community, locality, rustic, petty-bourgeois, specific locales, quaint little houses and rooms of the town, sleepy streets.
	Public Square	Dynamic, crowd, forum, metropolitan, the internal externalized (the private/intimate becomes public), theatrical (place of the clown, the rogue, the fool).
	Distortion	Elsewhere, miraculous, bewitched, dreams, hallucinations.
	Metanarrative	For sections of text without a concrete sense of space, which could be internal (e.g. commentary, direct address to the reader) or external (e.g. glosses, framing statements, contained texts; authorial/editorial notes, etc) to the narrative. See metatextual / paratextual / intratextual connection types.

The marked-up text as an XML file is processed using a series of functions written in the Python programming language then exported as a gexf. file and imported into Gephi, a standard tool for visualising and analysing graphs (see Online Methodological Appendix for a full account). The program generates not a single map but a map series with different aspects of spatio-temporal meaning prioritised in each (see Table 4). A force-based algorithm (ForceAtlas 2) generates the shape of the visualisation in black and white. Finally, the topological form is exported as a graphml.file for final visual styling in colour with names and symbology in Adobe Illustrator. The final visualisations can be presented with curved or straight connections as desired.

Table 2 Connection types and styles

Symbol	Name	Description
————	Direct	Where frames are physically connected and the narrative shifts seamlessly between two related topoi.
············	Indirect	Where topoi which are not immediately reachable from the current frame are referenced. E.g. points viewed from afar.
- - -	Projection	Where the narrative movement is conducted through imagination, memory, dreams, etc.
– – – –	Interrupt	Where the narrative movement reverts to a previous state after a tangent or diversion.
— — —	Jump	Where the narrative movement is disconnected or broken by interrupts.
....	Metatextual	Where the narrative refers externally to a pre-existing work.
. . . .	Paratextual	Where the narrative contains a sub-narrative that is linked but could be separated from it.
– · – · –	Intratextual	Where the narrative addresses the reader directly or draws attention to its own fictionality.

Table 3 Chronotopic Cartography colour key

Chronotopes		Connections	
☁	Anti-Idyll	————	Direct
🏰	Castle	············	Indirect
?	Distortion	– – – –	Interrupt
⇅	Encounter	— — —	Jump
☀	Idyll	- - - -	Projection
📖	Metalepsis	....	Metatextual
🪑	Parlour	. . . .	Paratextual
🏪	Public Square	– · – · –	Intratextual
🛣	Road		
🚪	Threshold		
🏘	Provincial Town		
🌲	Wilderness		

Table 4 Map types generated from the mark-up

Map format	Description
Complete	A full map of a text showing the topoi (nodes), their associated toporefs (place names referenced also as a node), and the connections between them (arrowed lines)
Topoi	This shows the topoi (framenames) and the connections between them privileged over the chronotopes and without the associated toporefs
Syuzhet	This shows the topoi and their connections as they appear sequentially across the text in the order in which the tale is told
Fabula	Corresponding to the 'Syuzhet', the 'Fabula' map shows the topoi and connections in the order in which events actually occurred (not the order as told)
Topoi and chronotopic archetypes	This shows the relationship between the topoi and the underlying chronotopic types. For many texts this graph appears as disconnected clusters. However, where topoi change chronotope over the course of a text when a place changes identity (e.g. an 'Idyll' becomes a 'Castle'), the clusters become interlinked
Chronotopic archetypes and toporefs	This shows the relationship between the core chronotopic form and the toporefs nested within them
Deep chronotope	This is the simplest map to understand. It represents each chronotope as a single node, with the scale reflecting the percentage of the text dedicated to each and how they relate to one another

CORE TOPOLOGIES

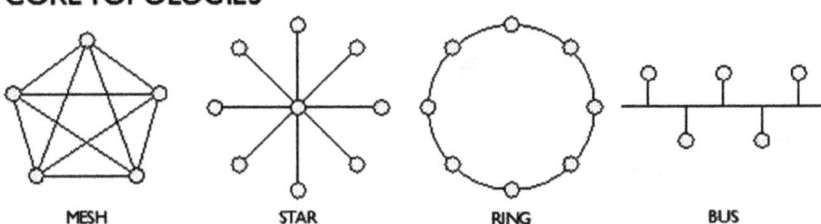

HYBRID TOPOLOGIES

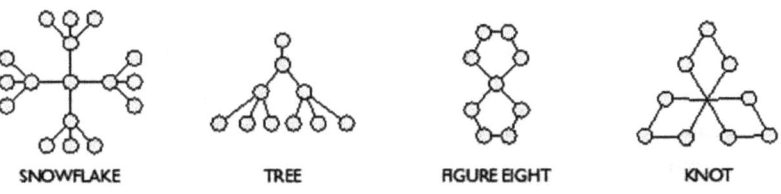

Figure 2 Topological forms (image created by Duncan Hay).

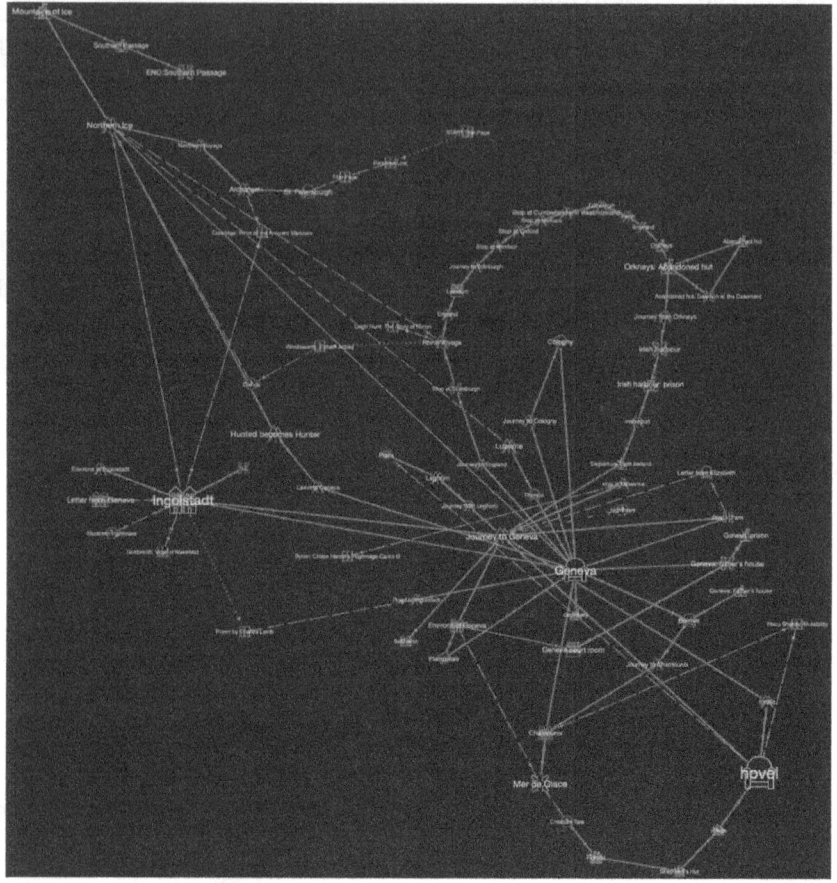

Figure 3 Topoi map for *Frankenstein* showing ring topology. Image from Chronotopic Cartographies project. No permission required here and elsewhere.

What emerged from visualising texts as graph networks was a variety of topological shapes that essentially provided a 'map' of the underlying spatial form of the narrative (see Figure 2). The base topologies of 'Mesh', 'Star', 'Ring', and 'Bus' also sometimes combined to form more complex entities such as 'Snowflake' or 'Figure of Eight'. As comparable forms began to emerge across texts, the team realised that if we could find a way to 'read' the topological forms in relation to narrative structure and meaning, then an integrated visual-verbal method for analysis would follow from this.

It is worth looking briefly at an example to understand the comparative potential of literary topology more fully. In a ring topology, a circle is formed in which each node is connected only to the two nodes on either side of it. What this suggests, as a spatial form for literature, is a strong linearity within the narrative, or a clear journey out away from home and back. This ring form appears very distinctively as a 'Big Wheel' in the Topoi map for Mary Shelley's *Frankenstein* (Figure 3).[14] Here it relates directly to the spatial practices of Victor Frankenstein as narrator and strongly emphasises his movement as 'touristic' for much of the narrative after his meeting with the Creature on the *Mer de Glace*. Victor sets off on a Grand Tour of Europe with his friend Clerval, that is really a trip to the remotest point (an abandoned hut on Orkney) to try and make a mate for the Creature, at his command (shown top right as a small triangle off the loop).

So, in the case of *Frankenstein*, a series of stops at popular tourist destinations on that ring (e.g. Oxford; Matlock; and Cumberland and Westmorland) is actually a driven trajectory that ultimately goes round on itself and leads nowhere. This also points to deeper conflicting motives in Victor himself and multiple levels of denial about his own actions and responsibilities for them. In his explanation for the tour, Victor deliberately misleads his father: 'I expressed a wish to visit England; but, concealing the true reasons of this request I clothed my desires under the guise of wishing to travel and see the world' (Shelley, [1818], 1996: 109). The given reason (to himself) for Victor's overtly elaborate movement is to hide his motivation from his family. But the true reason is to delay the inevitable. Thus, although the spatial dominates, the underlying motivation is temporal.[15] By the end, the entire structure functions as a kind of parody of the whole purpose of undertaking the Grand Tour that should refine the gentleman and turn the boy into a man: Clerval is dead and Victor's future is doomed. Here, visualising the text proves extremely effective in revealing spatial tensions.

Multiple ring topologies also appear in the Topoi map of H. G. Wells's *The War of the Worlds* (see Figure 4). The largest of these (top right) concerns the narrator's attempts to survive a Martian invasion by fleeing the capital. He moves through specific areas around central London (Hampton Court; Twickenham, Richmond) and eventually back through Wimbledon to Waterloo Bridge, right in the centre of the city. At the top of the loop, in a way directly comparable to Victor's, a small sub-loop occurs at 'Sheen: the ruined house' where the narrator is trapped underneath a Martian invasion pod that has landed on top of him (see Figures 5 and 6).

We would not normally read these two texts together since they are not of the same literary period or genre. However, when we do juxtapose them – led by the underlying topological form – we can see that actually they *do* have quite a lot in

---

[14] For any single marked-up text a map series is generated rather than a single map, with each map form privileging a different aspect of spatial meaning. See Online Methodological Appendix for a full account.

[15] For a fuller reading of the *Frankenstein* topologies, see Bushell et al., 2022b.

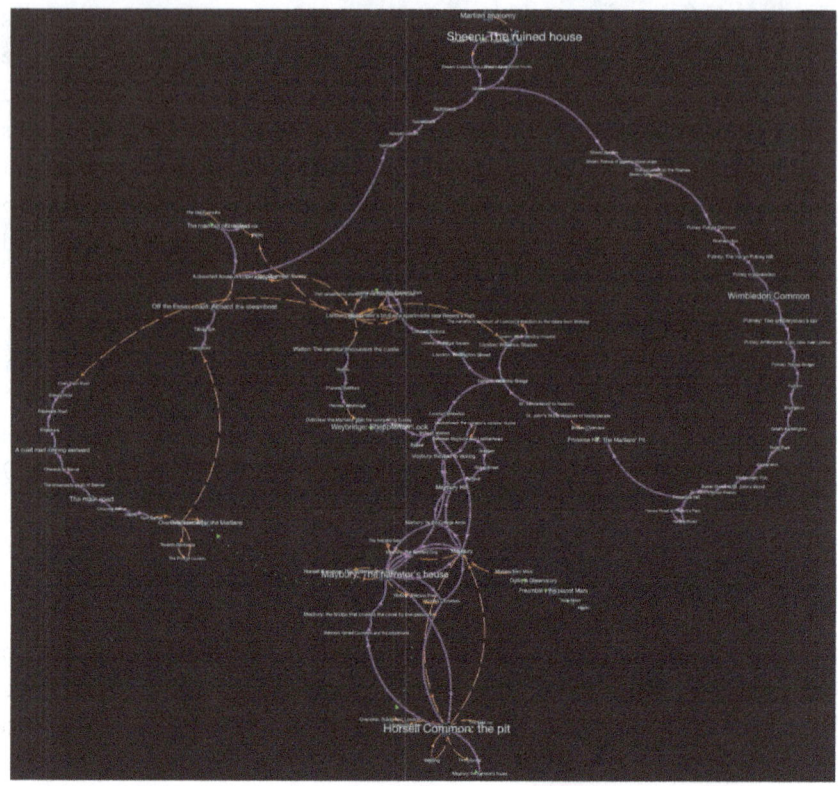

Figure 4 Topoi map for *The War of the World* showing multiple rings.

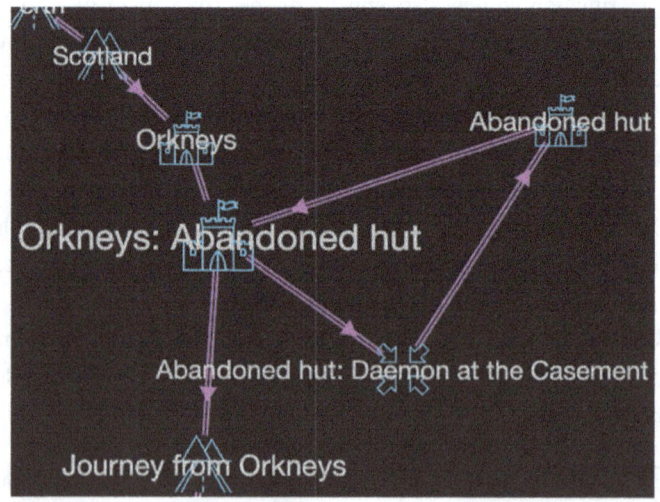

Figure 5 Detail from *Frankenstein*.

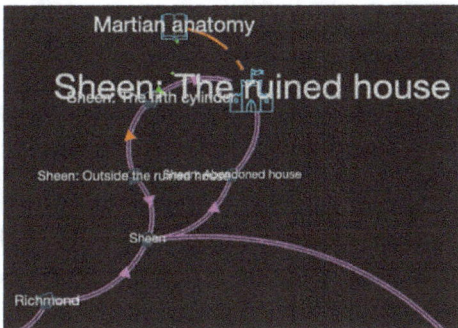

Figure 6 Detail from *The War of the World*.

common. For example, in both texts human motives, actions, and movement are extreme, driven by strong external force – which is what generates the ring topologies. The nature of that external agency is hostile and alien, resulting in forms of movement by compulsion and against the will of the narrator. This is in strong contrast to the power of the spatial catalysts themselves. In *Frankenstein*, the Creature seems to appear and disappear at will and can travel and inhabit the most remote regions; in *The War of the Worlds*, the Martians are (initially) immobile but even in this condition are all-powerful (the narrator is forced to remain hidden at the ruined house in Sheen). Taken even further, we can see that grouping texts according to topology rather than to period or genre might create an *entirely alternative way of spatialising literature* or of reading texts through their spatial forms.

Valuing Subjectivity: A Shropshire Lad

We want to conclude this first section of the Element by considering the value of manual versus automated mark-up and of foregrounding inherent subjectivity within digital literary mapping, because this is crucial to the larger argument concerning a different way of doing things for the Humanities. Privileging manual, subjective mark-up goes directly against a dominant DH desire to automatise reading processes in the Humanities (using tools such as Named-Entity Recognition, Natural Language Processing, and so on). The whole rationale for 'reading' in and through a computer is to undertake tasks beyond the capacity of a human reader. This is why the argument for scale (and thus 'distance') is so powerful. But a desire to find ways of applying a fully automated model to a subject like Literary Studies assumes a singularity of meaning, or at least an easily defined spectrum. This is, again, fundamentally at odds with the object of scrutiny (complex language) which, by its very nature, is resistant to the reduction to singularity. Thus, rather than seeking to drive towards an absolute, fully automated method we suggest the need for a counterbalancing force that seeks to uncover the implicit subjectivity held in that supposedly objective process.

Is there anything *wrong* in admitting that each individual coder will generate a subtly different map? When we code manually, and in a way that allows room for the subjectivity of the coder in relation to the text, the same text can produce different visualisations through the mark-up. Subjective decision-making is an innate part of coding and the more complex and rich the text – as for the field of Literary Studies – the greater likelihood there is of variation. This is only a problem if the goal of digital literary mapping is to create universal automated tools with the aim of producing the same results for any user. If the purpose of the exercise is to create digital tools that can be integrated with textual criticism to create complex and multiple interpretations, then this is surely unproblematic. Each critic will come up with a distinctive reading, so why should it not be the case that each map-maker comes up with a distinctive map form?[16]

In the *Chronotopic Cartographies* project, the spatial schema requires the coder to chunk out the text according to its chronotopic identity, but this identity is far from absolute. Certain chronotopes such as 'threshold', for example, are not absolutely determined and could easily be defined in different ways. Equally, chronotopes are themselves innately dialogic. Deciding where one chronotopic identity ends and the next begins is another subjective judgement. In the course of coding literary time-space we also found that prior familiarity with the text was essential (it was far more difficult to make such choices for a text that had not been read before). This suggests that the act of coding is itself interpretative, involving a particular kind of anticipatory momentum.

The example we end with here – A. E. Housman's poem *A Shropshire Lad* – displays the subjective judgement of two different coders using the *Chronotopic Cartographies* schema with strongly distinctive resulting visualisations.[17] Across the map series for this text, some of the maps made by the two coders look quite similar (e.g. the underlying Deep Chronotope map), while others look very different (Complete map, Topoi map, and Syuzhet map). For the rest of this section we seek to explore why this might happen, how interpretation acts upon mark-up if the base text is not simply treated as 'data' by a computer, and why this might be worth retaining or playing off against automated results.

---

[16] Cf. Reuschel et al., 2013, in which they compare the results of ten groups of students making literary maps for Schiller's *William Tell* (145–46).

[17] James Butler (RA on the *Chronotopic Cartographies* project) was the initiating force here in suggesting marking the text up twice by different readers.

Some context is required. *A Shropshire Lad* was published by Housman in 1896. The long poem consists of sixty-three short simple lyric sections written in a loose ballad form. A strong sense of mortality underlies the whole and this sense of loss, combined with its depiction of the composite 'lad' of the title in the full flush of youth (shepherd; farmhand; new recruit; soldier; doomed youth), made the poem extremely popular during the First World War (which it strangely anticipated). As Nick Laird puts it: 'if Housman were an emotion then, he would be longing' (Housman, [1896] 2010: xiv).

In the text, person and place are bound together but temporality is often at odds with spatiality. It is as if the narrator is out of step with his own time. So place is both real and remembered, lived and allegorical, present and past, as in the distilled perfection of poem XL:

> Into my heart an air that kills
> From yon far country blows:
> What are those blue remembered hills,
> What spires, what farms are those?
>
> That is the land of lost content,
> I see it shining plain,
> The happy highways where I went
> And cannot come again.
> (Housman, [1896] 2010: 51)

The poem's sense of place means that, across the whole sequence, it repeatedly circles away and back to key sites (Wenlock Edge, Ludlow Tower, and Bredon Hill) in a way that lends itself to the musical treatments it has received by Vaughan Williams and others. At the same time, this circular structure is offset by a model of accumulation. Housman himself described the writing of poetry as cumulative: 'a secretion ... like turpentine in the fir ... like the pearl in the oyster' (Housman, [1896] 2010: 255). He continues:

> As I went along, thinking of nothing in particular, only looking at things around me and following the progress of the seasons, there would flow into my mind ... sometimes a line or two of verse, sometimes a whole stanza at once, accompanied, not preceded, by a vague notion of the poem which they were destined to form part of. ([1896] 2010: 255)

So we might say that the structure of *A Shropshire Lad* inherently holds within it two different ways of responding: in terms of an accumulation of small scenes and moments that add up to more than the sum of their parts, or as a timeless whole, with motifs flowing and repeating across it.

When we turn to the decisions made by each coder, resulting in dramatically different visualisations, we can see this doubleness in play. Perhaps subconsciously

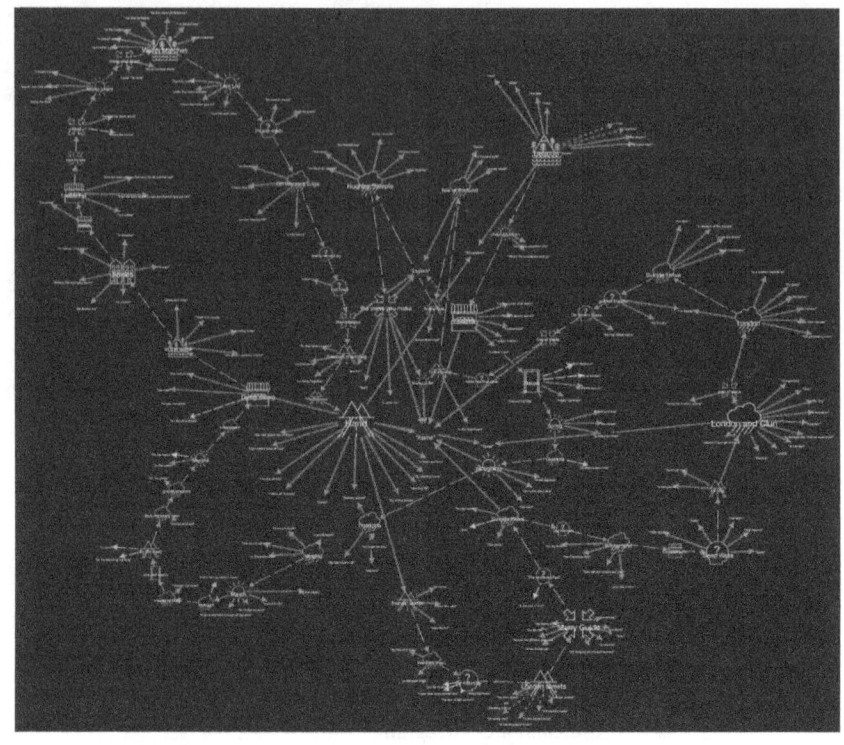

Figure 7 Complete map for *A Shropshire Lad* (Coder 1).

New Approaches for Digital Literary Mapping 27

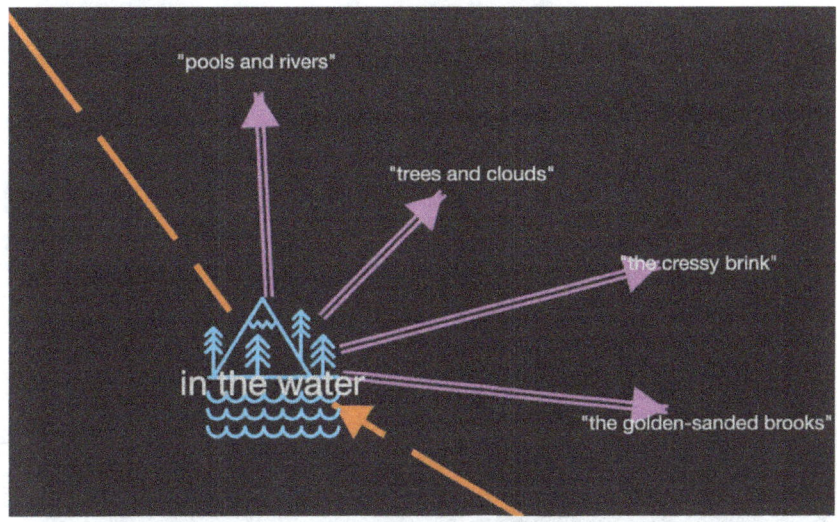

Figure 8 Detail from Complete map for *A Shropshire Lad* (Coder 1).

Figure 9 Detail from Complete map for *A Shropshire Lad* (Coder 1).

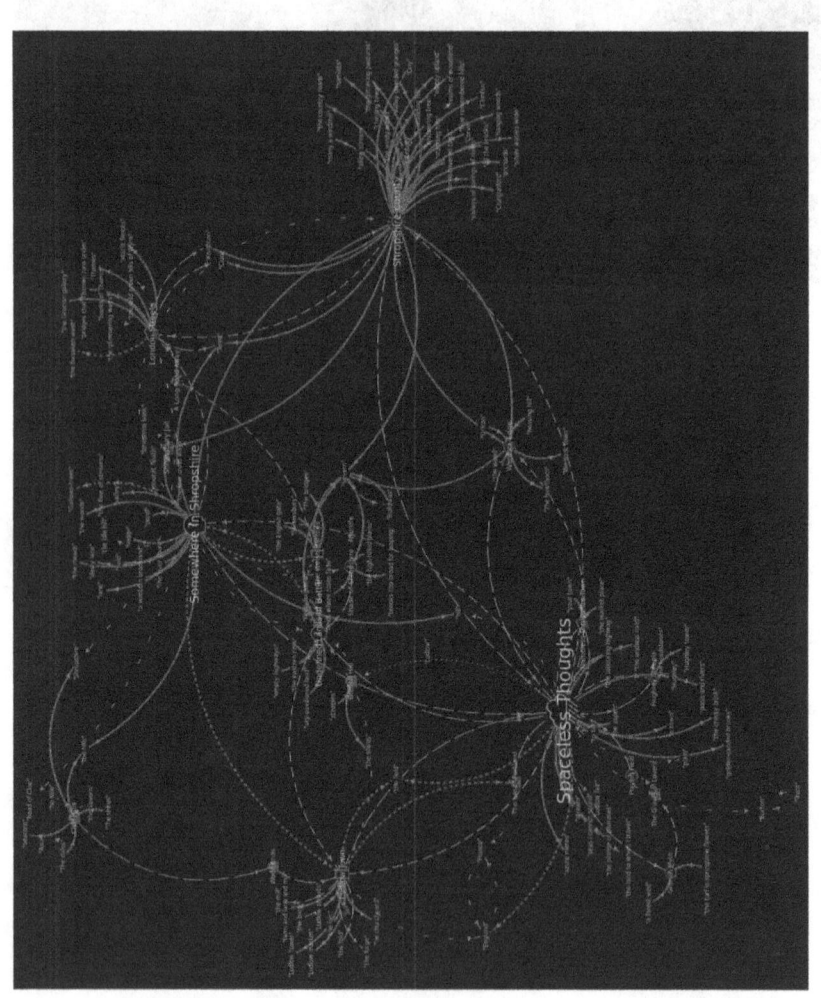

Figure 10 Complete map for *A Shropshire Lad* (Coder 2).

New Approaches for Digital Literary Mapping 29

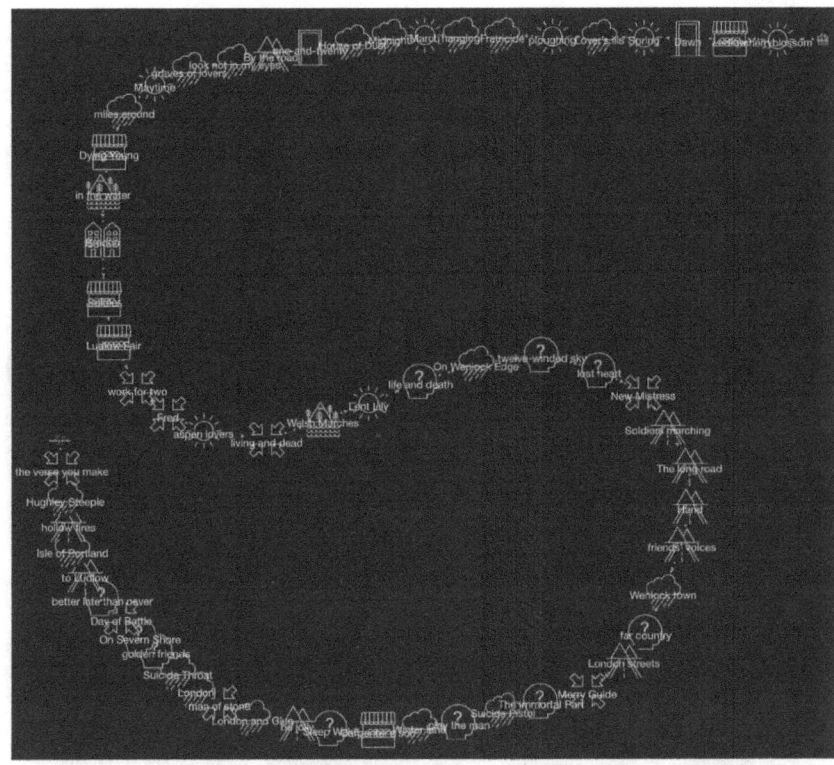

Figure 11 Syuzhet map for *A Shropshire Lad* (Coder 1).

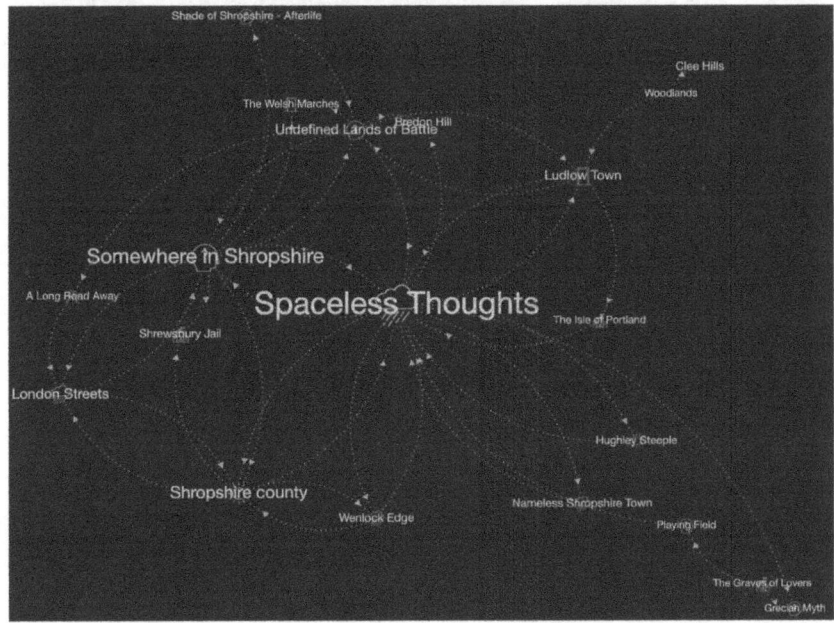

Figure 12 Syuzhet map for *A Shropshire Lad* (Coder 2).

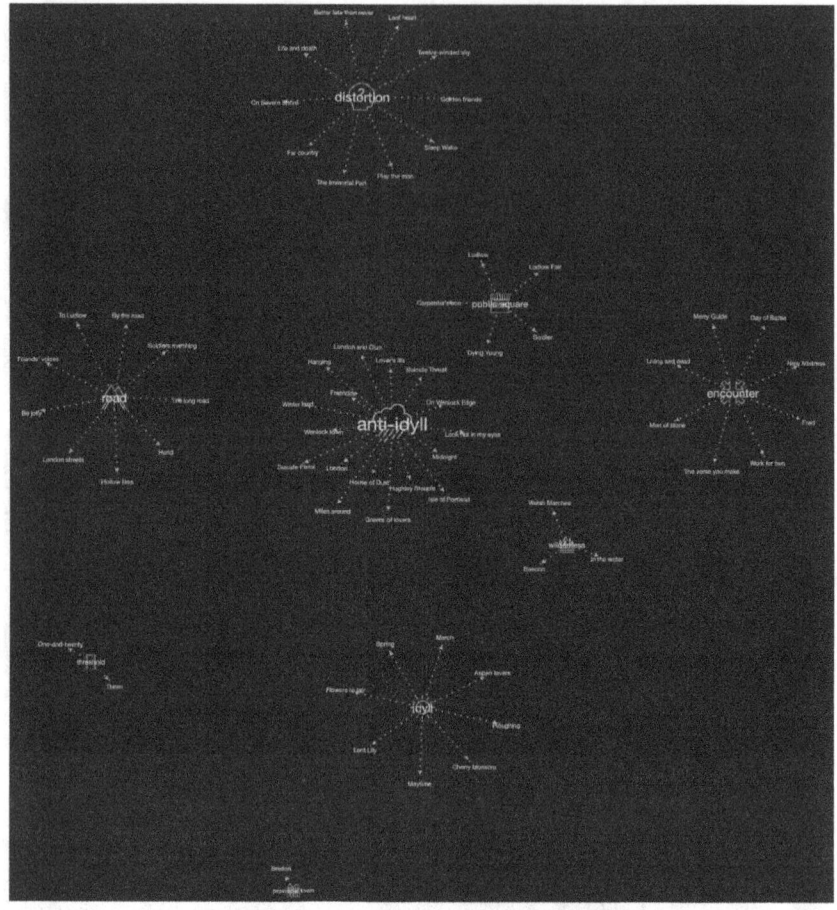

Figure 13 Chronotopes and Topoi map for *A Shropshire Lad* (Coder 1).

New Approaches for Digital Literary Mapping 31

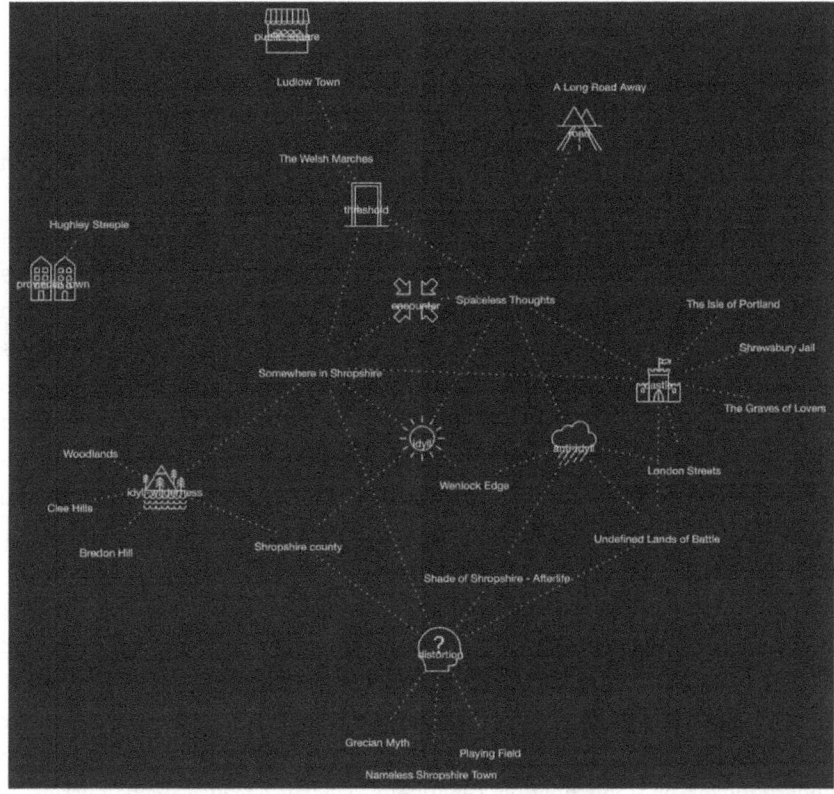

Figure 14 Chronotopes and Topoi map for *A Shropshire Lad* (Coder 2).

Coder 1 (Bushell) felt a greater need to respect the poem's underlying compositional history, whereas Coder 2 (Butler) responded more directly to the experience of reading the published text. At any rate, Coder 1's maps treat each short poem as a separate 'place'. On the butterfly form of the Complete map (Figure 7) this results in small space-specific clusters for particular poem sites. The effect of her mark-up and map 'style' is to create small spatial clusters around the dominant topoi that almost read as poems themselves and form loops of connected meaning. So, for example, 'in the water' contains 'pools and rivers', 'trees and clouds', 'the cressy brink', and 'the golden-sanded brooks' (see Figure 8). Where the underlying chronotope is internal and thus of the mind (distortion), this is felt even more strongly, as if the actual places spring from the imagination. Perhaps the best example of this is 'Far Country' as a poem about the narrator's own youth with the related toporefs of: 'yon far country', 'those blue remembered hills', 'the land of lost content', and 'happy highways' (see Figure 9).

In contrast, Coder 2 coded the text as if it were a single continuous whole by determining universal spatial areas (see Figure 10). The map shows the coalescence of several conceptual representations of Shropshire with greater and lesser degrees of specificity. Names for chronotopic spaces reflect the poem's spatio-temporal identity with a sense of the real being rendered abstract: 'Somewhere in Shropshire', 'Shropshire County', and 'Spaceless Thoughts'.

The Syuzhet maps (showing the order of events as narrated) are the point at which the two coders are most divergent (see Figures 11 and 12). Coder 1's unusual map form is created by the fact that, for her, the poem moves forward in a series of steps which create a chain of linkage but represent distinct moments in time, suspended as linked memories. The figure S ('S' for Syuzhet?) is a pleasing coincidence created by the graph algorithm. In Coder 2's Syuzhet map, despite all the place specificity of the poem, 'Spaceless Thoughts' lie at its heart. The poem's structure is visualised as a series of interconnected and intermingling memory pockets expressed through a narrator who lies outside the spaces and times being recounted.

One other map that emerges as highly distinctive is that which shows the connectedness of the underlying chronotopes (see Figures 13 and 14). Although Coders 1 and 2 identified similar deep chronotopic structures beneath the poem, Coder 1's privileging of the poetic spaces of each mini-text within the whole generates the hybrid topological form of a snowflake structure with each underlying chronotope floating separately. This is because each location is assumed to only ever relate to one spatio-temporal form. Here the anti-idyll predominates, with eighteen frames linked to this chronotope. The sense in which the imagination of the narrator/persona determines the mood and content is also felt in the dominance of both anti-idyll and distortion. In Coder 2's comparable visualisation, places are far more dynamic in relation to the chronotopes because one place changes its chronotopic identity across the whole. The idyll form again predominates. But now 'Wenlock Edge' is both idyll *and* anti-idyll, while 'Shropshire County' is at different times an idyll wilderness, an idyll and 'a remembered place'. Again this reflects a subjective judgement about the nature of spatiality in relation to poetic form.

We have chosen to conclude Section 1 with this example since it so clearly illustrates the point we seek to make: that when we value the process as well as the product of map-making then multiplicity and difference in the maps generated by two coders (marking up manually from the same text) is not something to be hidden or silently omitted. However, we also acknowledge that this raises further questions. We have shown how different choices in manual mark-up can result in very different visualisations; but what of the point of connection between text and image – the underlying algorithm that generated the maps?

In Gephi, four different types of algorithm emphasise different features of the topology (differences, complementarities, ranking and geographic repartition). For the project, the team used the Gephi algorithm 'Force Atlas 2' as standard, because it was designed to 'spatialise small world, scale-free networks' and emphasise complementarities. There was a logical reason to choose *this* algorithm for *this* task, but it was still one choice amongst three force-directed algorithms (Force Atlas, Fruchterman-Reingold, and Yifan Hu).

If we generate the Complete map for *A Shropshire Lad* using *each* algorithm in Gephi (see Figures 15–17), we can see that Force Atlas and Yifan Hu produce similar forms but Fruchterman-Reingold is radically different (because it 'stimulates the graph as a system of mass particles'[18]). This reminds us that the nature of the algorithm bears directly upon interpretation and that it is essential to have a good understanding of the point of handover from human to machine.

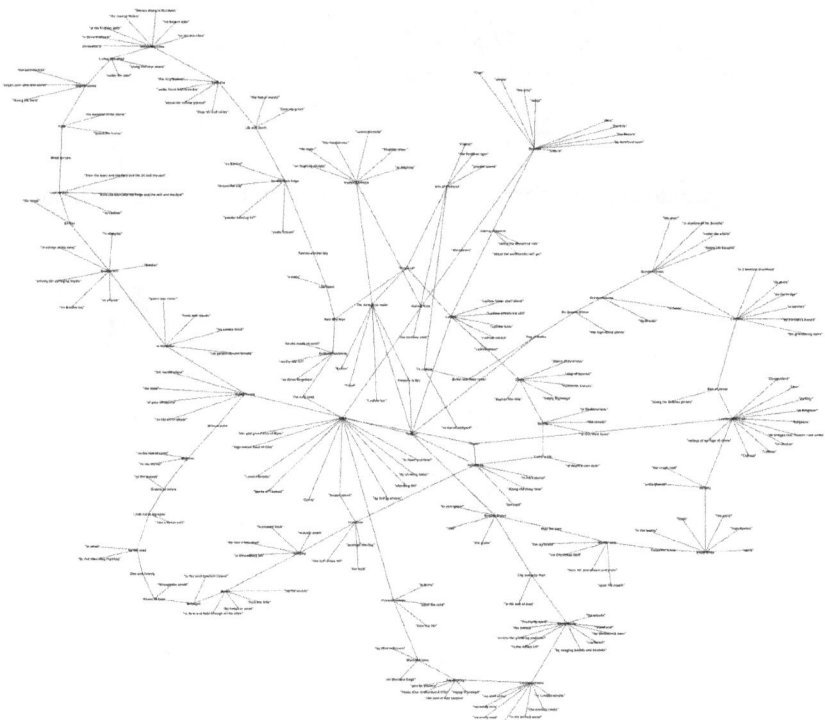

Figure 15 Complete map for *A Shropshire Lad* using Force Atlas 2 in Gephi.

---

[18] Gephi Tutorial Layouts', 2011. https://gephi.org/tutorials/gephi-tutorial-layouts.pdf; see also Online Methodological Appendix.

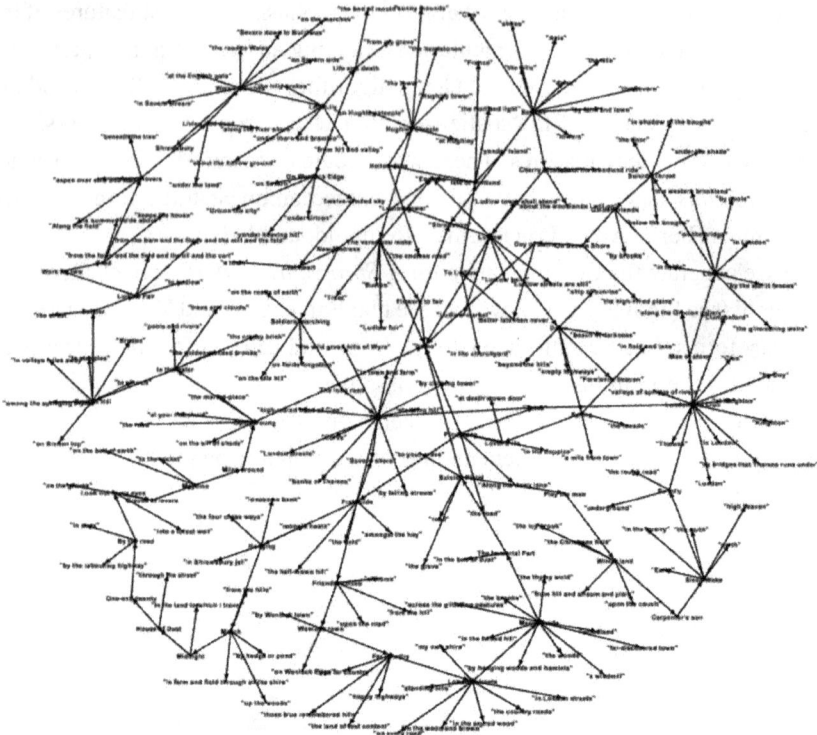

Figure 16 Complete map for *A Shropshire Lad* using Fruchterman-Rheingold in Gephi.

New Approaches for Digital Literary Mapping

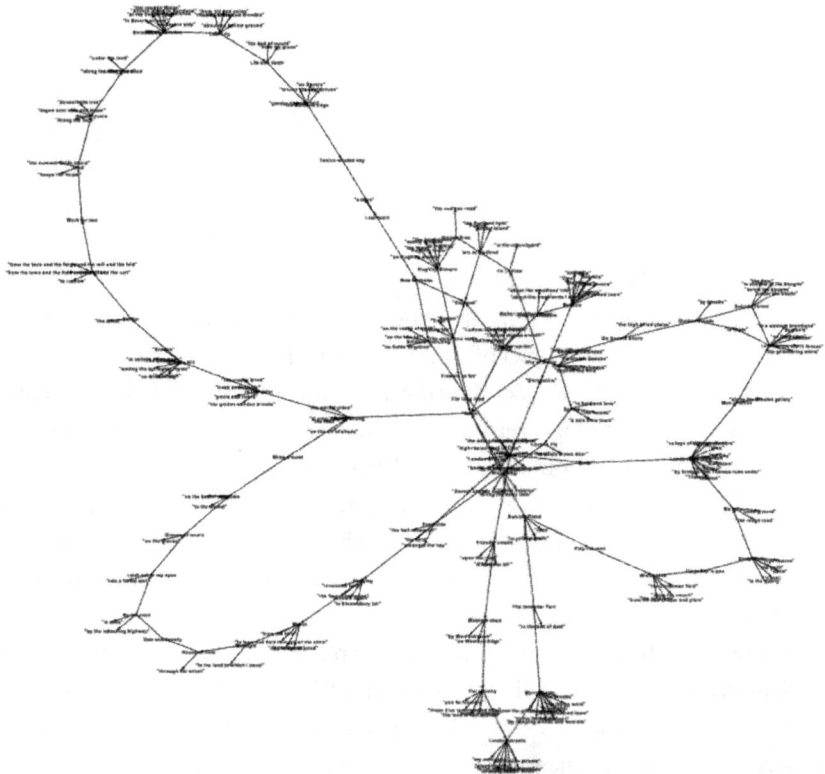

Figure 17 Complete map for *A Shropshire Lad* using Yi Fan Hu in Gephi.

As any cartographer knows, the most important skill in making a map is the act of selection – indeed, this is what allows the movement of critical cartography to read *against* the map in terms of what is not shown/what is hidden. This creates a paradox in which for the map to be of use it must always be a partial misrepresentation. The same is true for digital literary mapping. If every visualisation were displayed in every possible variant, the information would be overwhelming. We might say that just as a literary critic can choose those passages from a text which best support the reading being advanced, so the digital literary mapper can select the most telling map. But at the same time, in both cases, there is a danger of distortion by omission. At the very least we need to be aware of this.

2 Back to Bakhtin: Understanding and Applying a Chronotopic Method

> We cannot help but be strongly impressed by the representational importance of the chronotope. Time becomes ... palpable and visible. ... An event can be communicated, it becomes information, one can give precise data on the place and time of its occurrence.
>
> (Bakhtin, [1937] (1984): 250)

Section 1 established a larger context for literary mapping in the digital domain and the need for new tools and methods for DH scholars that can meet the complex demands of the object of study. Section 2 focusses on the usefulness of mapping time and space in a combined way for literature through the concept of the chronotope using tools created for the *Chronotopic Cartographies* project. The concept is derived from the work of Russian theorist, Mikhail Bakhtin. The first half of this section makes clear the degree to which the digital method is indebted to his account of the chronotope in his famous essay, 'Forms of Time and of the Chronotope in the Novel,' and the usefulness of this in providing a new way forward for digital mapping more broadly.

At the same time, in this section we explore the challenge that literary realism presents to digital literary mapping by adopting two approaches to Charles Dickens's *Oliver Twist*. We map realism both in the way it obviously invites – by absolute mapping onto the real with literary place treated as correspondent – and by mapping chronotopically using graph topologies generated out of the text. We do so in order to highlight the problems involved when assuming direct correspondence between the geographic and the fictional but also to show that absolute and relative forms of mapping are not mutually exclusive.

Why Go Back to Bakhtin?

At the close of his well-known essay on 'Forms of Time and of the Chronotope', Bakhtin reasserts the fundamental importance of time and space for literature:

> [meanings] must take on the *form of a sign* that is audible and visible for us (a hieroglyph, a mathematical formula, a verbal or linguistic expression, a sketch). Without such temporal-spatial expression, even abstract thought is impossible. (Bakhtin, [1937] 1984: 252).

It is only through *visualisation*, by making the abstract material, that spatio-temporal meaning can be fully understood. Such a statement anticipates and to some extent validates the literary mapping approach adopted by the *Chronotopic Cartographies* team. In his essay (and in many other writings stretching over a fifty-year period) Bakhtin set about devising an alternative view from that of his fellow formalists, opposing the idea that the Humanities can best be understood by means of larger patterns and structures and seeking to develop a model generated out of the text and contextualising literature through the filter of real-world constructs.

Bakhtin consistently approaches the text (form and content) in terms of what is unique to literature rather than to linguistics or philosophy. The text is not reduced to a reflection of something else. This is why, in our view, the chronotope is a more useful and pliable model than other time/space combinations, such as Lefebvre's tertiary space (1974), Foucault's heterotopia (1986), or Harvey's time-space compression (1989). Unlike these models, the chronotope is specifically identified with *literature* and the unique spatio-temporal constructs it generates.

Ostensibly, the emergence of the chronotope could be seen to correspond to a more general turning towards space at the end of the twentieth century. However, it is missing from many influential accounts by major commentators such as Soja, Jameson, and Massey, none of whom mention it explicitly.[19] As Susan Friedman explains, 'Bakhtin's sense of the mutually constitutive and interactive nature of space and time in narrative has largely dropped out of narrative poetics' (2008: 194). One reason for this oversight may be that critical history has tended to dwell upon the *temporal* elements of the chronotope. Bakhtin himself prioritises the temporal over the spatial – after all, the title of his essay is 'Forms of *Time*' not space and he asserts that 'the primary category of the chronotope is time' (Bakhtin, [1937] 1984: 85). In Bakhtin's account, protagonists are defined by their 'eventness', and his analysis is influenced by the temporally orientated narrative distinction between *fabula/syuzhet* of Russian Formalism (chronological order of events versus order of the narrative as related).

From this perspective, the chronotope appears as a confirmation of the very impulse *against* which the spatial turn was turning. What is elided, however, in the accounts of Bakhtin's chronotope that focus on time at the expense of space, is the fundamental interconnectivity of the two. Friedman makes this point well in her Kristevan reading of Bakhtin's 'spatial tropes' where she explicitly rejects reading for either time or space *alone* (1993: 12–23). The chronotope, in Friedman's understanding, is valuable for its delineation of narrative axes which allow the reader – occupying the vertical axis – to interact with the text's horizontal axis, connecting these times and spaces inside and outside the text. Our method, which moves iteratively between the process of reading and

---

[19] See Jameson, 1990; Massey, 1994; and Soja, 1996.

mapping texts chronotopically and the product of synchronic visualisations, shares this intersection of the linear and the simultaneous.

One person who certainly *does* recognise the value of Bakhtin in relation to space is Franco Moretti. He cites Bakhtin only a few times in *Atlas of the European Novel* but those moments are worth close consideration. In a discussion of spatial organisation (centres and margins) in the historical novel, Moretti quotes Bakhtin directly (embedding the latter's words within his own):

> The chronotope in literature has an intrinsic generic significance. It can even be said that it is precisely the chronotope that defines genre and generic distinctions.
>
> Each genre possesses its own space, then, – and each space its own genre: defined by spatial distribution – by a map – which is unique to it. (Moretti, 1998: 35)

As the quotation he provides makes clear, the inherent power of Bakhtin's model lies in the way in which it spatialises genre. Moretti comes directly out of this to develop his own approach in terms of the explicit visualisation of those spatial elements by means of mapping activities 'as analytical tools: that dissect the text in an unusual way, bringing to light relations that would otherwise remain hidden' (1998: 3). As Moretti himself explicitly states, 'Bakhtin's essay on the chronotope ... is the greatest study ever written on space and narrative, and it doesn't have a single map' (2005: 79). In other words, there is a sense in which Moretti's maps are nothing more nor less than *a visualisation of the theory of the chronotope.*

For example, Moretti's focus on the picaresque novel looks directly back to Bakhtin's description of the development of the novel in relation to the chronotope of the road. If we look at what Bakhtin himself does, we find that he historicises and identifies changing usage and meaning of 'the road' over time and across generic categories. He tells us that 'in folklore a road is almost never merely a road, but always suggests the whole, or a portion of "a path of life"', and he contrasts this with an earlier Greek romance model where 'it was merely a mannered enchaining of coordinates both spatial (near/far) and temporal (at the *same* time/at *different* times)' (Bakhtin, [1937] 1984: 120). Later, when he returns to this subject in his 'Concluding Remarks', Bakhtin combines the predominantly *spatial* form of the road with the *temporal* form of 'the encounter'. He explains:

> Encounters in a novel usually take place 'on the road'. The road is a particularly good place for random encounters. On the road ... the spatial and temporal paths of the most varied people ... intersect at one spatial and temporal point. ... On the road the spatial and temporal series defining human fates and lives combine with one another. ... Time, as it were, fuses together with space and flows in it (forming the road). ([1937] 1984: 244)

New Approaches for Digital Literary Mapping 39

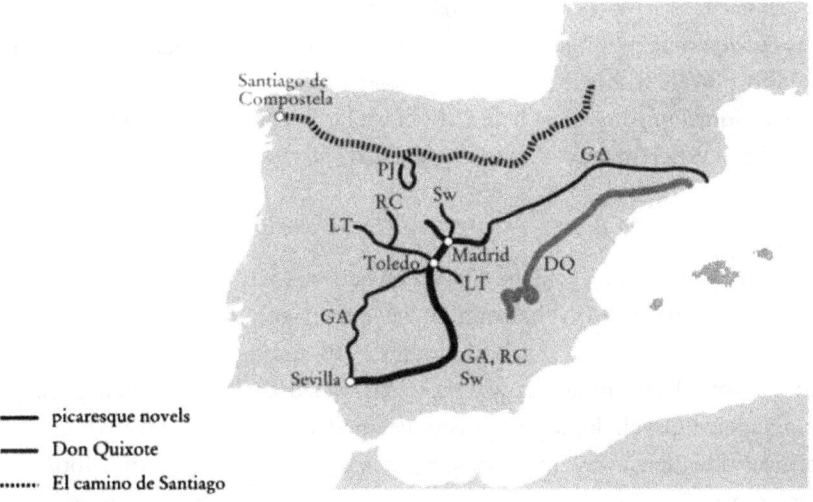

— picaresque novels
— Don Quixote
······ El camino de Santiago

Novels included:
GA Mateo Alemán *Guzmán de Alfarache*, I and II
LT anonymous *Lazarillo da Tormes*
PJ López de Ubeda *La picara Justina*
RC Miguel de Cervantes *Rinconete y Cortadilo*
Sw Francisco de Quevedo *The Swindler*

Figure 18 Spanish picaresque novels of the sixteenth and seventeenth centuries in *Atlas of The European Novel,* 49. Reproduced by kind permission of the author.

Moretti takes Bakhtin's account, acknowledges his influence indirectly by presenting a quotation from Bakhtin on the same page as the map, and then makes his *own* map that partially visualises the chronotope in relation to a particular sub-genre. His immediate aim is to contrast the pilgrimage route to the North with that of the picaresque novel, to make the point that 'these novels turn their back to the pilgrims of Camino de Santiago for roads that are much more worldly and crowded and wealthy' (Moretti, 1998: 48). The map makes this clear (see Figure 18). The secondary aim (also from Bakhtin) is to make the point that the novel form and genre itself emerges out of the rhythm and pace of the road:

> A slow and regular process, daily, tiresome, often banal. But such is precisely the secret of the modern novel ... modest episodes with a limited narrative value, and yet, never without *some* kind of value. (1998: 48–49)

When we look closely at Moretti, it is clear that whilst his way of literary mapping emerges from Bakhtin without explicitly stating this, it also limits what the chronotope has to offer, in part by its strong focus on the spatial at the expense of the temporal, but also in its focus on the chronotope at a macro-level (as the determinant of genre/spatial form) rather than as intrinsic to meaning at multiple levels within the text.

Has something been lost here? Might we be able to go 'Back to Bakhtin' and develop a different way of mapping the text?

Abstraction and Automation: The Limits of Formalism

Another way to understand the distinction between 'distant' and 'close' reading, and the importance of challenging the dominance of the former model in relation to DH, is to go back to around 1910 and the emergence of Russian Formalism. These proto-literary theorists argued against the (then-dominant) biographical/psychological and historical models of literary analysis by shifting critical attention away from the author and onto the underlying forms and structures of language. The importance of this for the newly emerging disciplinary identity of Literary Studies is clear:

> Before Formalism, literary studies revolved around other branches of knowledge, but the Formalists provided the discipline with its own center of gravity by insisting that it had a unique and particular object of enquiry. (Steiner, 2016: 245)

In close relation to advances in Semiotics and Linguistics, that recognised the autonomy of language and the necessity of distinguishing between sign and referent, the formalists focussed their efforts on identifying universal underlying structures for literature. Key figures such as Viktor Shklovsky and Roman Jakobson sought to escape from authorial approaches to literary analysis and privileged instead the unique meaning of the literary utterance. This in turn led them to search for deep universal structures at work within literature and unique to it – hence their interest in 'morphology' (derived from Goethe) as a means of breaking the subject of enquiry down into sub-structures and their functions. The fruition of such an approach can be seen in Victor Propp's *Morphology of the Folktale* (1928), with its focus on a universal traditional literary form for which core elements can easily be identified.

In Britain, these principles were paralleled to some degree (although with a retained adherence to psychology) with the emergence of I. A. Richards's *Practical Criticism* (1928) as an attempt to give the new discipline of English Literature greater credibility. As a moral philosopher, Richards's understanding of English Literature as a discipline was that it could only exist alongside and in relation to other disciplines. (In this he differed from Russian formalists before him, and American New Critics after him, but he still provides a vital link between the two.) Just as formalist approaches to the subject of enquiry align it to 'positivist empiricism – the reduction of facts to sensory data' (Steiner, 2016: 253), so Richards tried to justify and validate the discipline by creating 'scientific' ways of producing empirical data from the analysis of undergraduate readers of poetry. Richards's principles were then taken up in America in the 1940s and embodied in literary-critical works that sought to identify primary underlying patterns and formulas in texts in ways that clearly look back to Formalism. As a consequence of the isolation of the literary work from historical or other contexts and the privileging of its more formal elements, both Practical and New Critical approaches became centred on exploring unique intrinsic meaning as held in the use of language for 'literary' or 'poetic' expression. This is what is meant by the resulting interpretative method of close reading: a mode of high-level analysis and attention to elements (such as metaphor and symbol; rhythm and metre; ambiguity and paradox) that unite form and content to produce meaning in works of literature. Crucially, however, if this *was* a method back in the 1930s and 1940s, it is certainly not understood to be so today. Close reading is *a skill* – a necessary mode of attentive analysis to details of language and meaning that occurs in conjunction with historical, theoretical, and philosophical frames (the wheel turns full circle).

Moretti's account of distant reading and desire to develop a 'morphology' for literature is implicitly underpinned by early formalist attempts to respond to literature more scientifically. But – crucially – what this brief history has sought to show is that, although distant reading is defined against and in opposition to close reading, *both* practices find a *shared origin* in Formalism.

This is vitally important when we return to the question of how to digitise literature today, because it makes clear that there were always *two divergent ways* of applying those formalist principles: to *scientific* ends (capable of computation to reveal patterns or elicit data), *and* far more subjectively in combined understanding of language and form at multiple levels. If this was true in relation to Literary Studies in the 1920s and 1930s, it is also true of Digital Literary Studies in the 2020s. Distant reading seeks, like Formalism, to elicit core elements from across the whole, using digital tools not available to the formalists to make the scope of exploration for underlying universals far larger than they could have imagined, as well as automating it. But an alternative way of working with texts allowing for multiple scales and zooming in and out is *also* there – as Bakhtin himself was well aware.

Moretti's strong commitment to form over content deviates sharply from Bakhtin's own position which he doggedly defined as being at odds with Formalism (despite having much in common with the movement). Bakhtin argued that Formalism was essentially a branch of Linguistics and that, because of this, it had been led away from considering what made literature distinctive (his own primary interest). In an early essay, 'The Problem of Content, Material and Form', he argues that an overemphasis on the material aesthetics of verbal art derives from an uncritical adoption of the methodology of an 'auxiliary discipline' (Bakhtin, [1924] 1990: 257–325). To Bakhtin, Formalism – steered and informed by Linguistics – is reductive and scientific in its approach in ways that do not meet the needs of literary study. Furthermore, he opposed the ways in which Formalism also sought to separate form from, and privilege it over, content: 'ignoring content leads to a "material aesthetics" ... [and] the lack of understanding of historicity and change' (Bakhtin, [1974] 1986: 169). Rather, form 'embrace[s] content from *outside, externalises it* [and then] *embodies it*' ([1974] 1986: 282). In other words, form is precisely what should create and enable the fusion of literature with context and create unity: macro and micro should be connected.

Another problem with earlier Formalism (form alone) or traditional biographical or ideological readings (content alone) is that both misunderstand context – either by dismissing it altogether or by fixing it in time and place. What Bakhtin emphasises in his opposition to both is the *situatedness* of context; the author's job is to generate a concrete world that combines space and time in a meaningful way using narrative.

This leads us back to Bakhtin's theory of the chronotope as a spatio-temporal context (for the novel in particular), in part derived from real-world structures and events. Through the chronotope, via the artistic process of assimilation and appropriation, certain elements of time and space are redetermined and become literary and, as a result, cannot be relegated to formalist analysis: 'a literary work's artistic unity in the relationship to actual reality is defined by its chronotope' (Bakhtin, [1937] 1984: 243). Formal categories might suit poetry's extra-historical language but a new approach is needed for the novel – a form whose language is constructed via a complex, unfixed, and unfinished spatio-temporal interchange between the 'real, unitary and as yet incomplete historical world' and 'the represented world in the text' ([1937] 1984: 253). The emphasis here on the dialogic nature of the literary chronotope is important in relation to the mapping of texts onto real-world locations, as we shall see next.

Bakhtin's Account of the Chronotope

In 'Forms of Time and of the Chronotope in the Novel', Bakhtin accounts for the origins of the term in Einstein's Theory of Special Relativity, which essentially argues that time moves relative to the observer and that an object in movement experiences time differently from a static object. He states:

> The special meaning it has in relativity theory is not important for our purposes; we are borrowing it for literary criticism almost as a metaphor (almost, but not entirely). What counts for us is the fact that it expresses the inseparability of space and time. ([1937] 1984: 84)

What does Bakhtin mean when he describes the chronotope functioning 'almost as a metaphor ... but not entirely'? Partly this reflects his interest in grounding literary forms in real-world spatial structures and concepts as discussed in the previous section. Partly it looks back to the original scientific discovery (which re-determined the laws of physics to assert the possibility of two individuals experiencing the same event differently). Crucially it suggests that space and time are not understood as fixed absolutes and, more than this, that individual experience and perception of experience is bound up with them and that they are thus, at least partly, subjective. Bakhtin's famous definition of the chronotope also seems to draw on its scientific origins:

> Time ... thickens, takes on flesh, becomes artistically visible; likewise, space becomes charged and responsive to the movements of time, plot and history. This intersection of axes, and fusion of indicators characterizes the artistic chronotope. ([1937] 1984: 84)

Time 'thickens' and space 'becomes charged' once we realise that they are inseparable and bear upon each other.

Of the chronotope more generally, Bakhtin centres on three core functions: it determines genre and generic distinctions; it determines the image of man in literature; and art and literature are shot through with '*chronotopic values* of varying degree and scope' ([1937] 1984: 243, italics original). These three elements provide the central ways in which Bakhtin determines the master-chronotopes for five ancient macro-genres and their early developments in his study. Following Propp, he outlines a morphology of character, plot, incidents, and geographical background; but it is when he brings these conventional elements into the 'charge' of the chronotope (which fuses and synthesises, like the imagination itself) that he is able to offer a unified spatial account of genre. For each of his macro-generic categories, Bakhtin identifies a unifying temporal construct that can then be applied to all elements of the novel and traced down to the level of motif within it (see Table 5).

Table 5 Bakhtin's macro-generic categories

Macro-genre	Unifying chronotopic identity	Nature of hero	Emerging genres	Sub-chronotopic motifs within text
The Adventure-novel of ordeal	Chance; short temporal sequences	Passive	Greek romance; Scott's *Waverley*	Meeting; parting
The Adventure-novel of the everyday	Transformation; linearity with knots in it	Able to grow	C18th novel; *Robinson Crusoe*	The road; the encounter; the sea voyage
Biography/ Autobiography	Search for knowledge; course of whole life	Life of action/life of thought	Plato's *Dialogues*; *Confessions*	Steps; seeking path; soul's ascent
Folkloric	Historical inversion; outside time but *appears* contemporary; realistic fantastic	Realistic, contemporary	Medieval romance, for example Dante's *Inferno*	Enchanted groves, castles, 'other worlds'
Rabelaisian	Special, self-contained; local/native growth	Deceitful, simple, rebellious, individual	Picaresque novel, Parody, for example *Don Quixote*	Carnivalesque, public square, theatre, destruction and creation, body, high and low
Idyllic	Cyclical, unified, natural, contained	Cyclical, complete	Love idyll, pastoral, provincial novel, for example *Werther*	Destruction of the idyll, the natural world, labour/ agriculture

So, for example, the adventure novel of ordeal's unifying temporality is defined *against* that of everyday existence – it is an *extra*ordinary time rather than ordinary time. Adventure time is 'neither historical, quotidian, biographical, nor even biological and maturational. Action lies outside these sequences' (Bakhtin, [1937] 1984: 91). Instead it consists of 'a series of short segments' so that '[w]hat is important is to be able to escape, to catch up, to outstrip, to be or not to be in a given place at a given moment' ([1937] 1984: 91). Time in its turn then integrates with character and motive for action because 'initiative is handed over to chance' ([1937] (1984): 95) – the 'hero' is not in command of his or her own destiny. Thus, a larger temporal identity finds expression through a sequential form that maps onto the space and the extent of the novel as it unfolds through plot, character, action, and event. In Bakhtin's approach, time becomes a kind of central strand around which these elements are spun. It is not that literature takes time-space and explores multiple subjectivities (the obvious first-step response to the theory of relativity, and possible for, say, the realist novel) but that when time and space are understood to be fully combined they become greater than the sum of their two parts and generate a determining core for the form. What Bakhtin effectively does here is to redetermine genre spatio-temporally – defining literary type in terms of these attributes rather than other more traditionally formal elements.

Another useful and distinctive factor of Bakhtin's account (albeit one that allows for the concept of the chronotope to be generalised rather than fully grasped) is the way in which he not only attempts the macro-definition but also drills down into 'motifs' and even the constituent linguistic elements within the text. Discussing the macro-genre of the adventure novel of the everyday, for example, Bakhtin states:

> The most characteristic thing about this novel is the way it fuses the course of an individual's life [at its major turning points] with his actual spatial course or road. ([1937] 1984: 120)

The chronotope works as a kind of externalised imaginative force that unites form, content, and context – fusing the character in his or her historical time with a strong spatial form (the road) – to generate a powerful metaphorical/symbolic layer of meaning.

Mapping Realism: *Oliver Twist*

For the rest of this section we turn away from a theoretical account of the chronotope and towards its application to the mapping of literary place and space. The realist novel provides a fertile ground for chronotopic digital literary mapping for two reasons. The first is because the realist chronotope, which

Bakhtin defines as occupying 'a particular concrete and graphically visible position in space', negotiates a unique relationship *between* the fictional and the real. It is not, Bakhtin goes on to clarify, 'a matter of how artistically realistic the image may be' and 'in no way requires a precise geographical determination'; 'it strives not so much for internal verisimilitude as for an idea of it' (Bakhtin, [1974] 1986: 47). Bakhtin's account complicates the nature of realism in relation to the geographic and suggests that the realist novel poses a challenge to the mapping of it. Second, the complexity and richness of the realist novel means that it will inevitably contain numerous chronotopes and sub-chronotopes.

The remainder of Section 2 therefore explores the mapping of realism comparatively in relation to these two conceptions of realism's chronotopic value: in a macro sense as a fully realised concrete world that offers a sense of geographic totality, but one that is also characterised by multiple sub-chronotopic motifs occurring at different scales within it. It does so first by using standard digital literary mapping techniques to map Charles Dickens's *Oliver Twist* (1838) onto the particular time-space of Victorian London (whilst, with Bakhtin, problematising the assumed direct correspondence this involves). This is then set *against* a chronotopic mapping of the same text relatively, from within.

A thin membrane between the fictional and factual is essential for a socially motivated writer such as Dickens. Thus, his work is inherently dialogic – intentionally connecting the work of art to cultural and societal concerns of his time. From this perspective such a work could be defined as a 'documentary chronotope' to account for the perceived closeness this creates between literature and life.[20] Bemong, Borghart, & De Dobbeleer (citing Bart Keunen) define the 'documentary chronotope' as 'typical of nineteenth-century realism' in which 'the fictional world is meant to be perceived as a construction which is immediately recognisable for the reader because of its close, "documentary" resemblance to the extra-literary world' (Borghart and De Dobbeleer, 2010: 79). In this reading, the fictional world is viewed as secondary to the world it represents. The equation of realism and history, or historiography, sets up a hierarchy in which the fictional is there to serve the greater aims of historical truth. It is our contention, however, that literary place and space both feed off and problematise the relationship between real and represented places. Realism encourages the reader to elide the two, but any attempts to map the fictional world, rather than doing the same, need to be self-consciously aware of the tension between them.

Critical interest in Dickens's relationship to the city has traditionally involved uncovering the London he described. This pattern can be traced from early works

---

[20] Significantly, these reflections on the 'documentary chronotope' give more prominence to time – or history – over space in assessing the relationship between realism and the real, see Bemong, Borghart, & De Dobbeleer, 2010.

of literary tourism, such as Frederick G. Kitton's *The Dickens Country* (1905), through to Jeremy Tambling's *Going Astray*, which deploys literary geography to trace Dickens through London (Tambling, 2009: 268). To Julian Wolfreys, such forms of 'biographical-historical reading' constitute a 'misunderstanding': 'problems can arise if one treats the subject's encounter with the urban space in straightforward historical or contextual terms, seeking in the process to relate fictive or imaginary vision to that which is real, historically speaking' (Wolfreys, 2012: 12). The key consequence of uncomplicatedly equating the world of *Oliver Twist* with that of early nineteenth-century London is that it risks prioritising the text's referential sites and de-prioritising the fictional. This impulse can be seen in Ruth Richardson's efforts to sequester the workhouse in 'a certain town' from its nested fictional location in order to align it with a historical place and conclude that 'the workhouse in which Oliver Twist was born *cannot be anywhere other than in central London*' (Richardson, 2015: 302, italics original). Reading in this way considerably distorts the text's literary spatiality.

It is time to return to the tools and methods of digital literary mapping. As stated in Section 1, we advocate a multiple and comparative model. A core anxiety for this kind of DH activity is that a lot of work produces little reward, and that the maps do not show us anything that was not already there.[21] However, the iterative method of visual–verbal interpretation that we advocate allows this charge to be easily combatted because the purpose is not to set one way of reading against another but to combine the two. By mapping literary realism across an author's work, or comparatively for different authors, certain patterns begin to emerge and we can understand more clearly exactly how realism functions.

We therefore decided to map *Oliver Twist* onto two maps of London. The first of these is the 1836 'Society for the Diffusion of Useful Knowledge' map, published cheaply for educational use. We chose this map because it is simple, legible, and almost exactly contemporaneous with the text. The second is Charles Booth's *Map of London Poverty* 1898–99.[22] Although a map of late nineteenth-century London, this map allows us to compare locations in the novel with areas of wealth and poverty in the city. Booth's map is colour coded, with the poorest regions represented in blue, dark blue, and black (see Figure 19). As we might expect, mapping *Oliver Twist* onto this base map shows Dickens's high-level knowledge of locations of poverty and crime in the city used in relation to the setting and characters.

---

[21] This anxiety (what did it show us that we did not already know?) is exemplified in Moretti's comment about his *Hamlet* network ('Did I really need it' [Moretti, 2011: 10]) – and repeatedly explored by Martin Paul Eve (2022: 105–107; 127).

[22] The map layer was created using the geovisualisation Memory Mapper tool created by Duncan Hay at UCL. Our thanks to LSE Library for providing the map data for the Booth base map.

Figure 19 Colour Key for Booth Map Series. BOOTH/E. Reproduced by kind permission of LSE archives.

Let's take an example of a mappable route to see how Dickens's realism works verbally and visually. For the section of the text when Oliver enters London with John Dawkins (the Artful Dodger) the route is narrated with great attentiveness to real place names in the first paragraph:

> As John Dawkins objected to their entering London before nightfall, it was nearly eleven o'clock when they reached the turnpike at Islington. They crossed from the Angel into St. John's Road; struck down the small street which terminates at Sadler's Wells theatre; through Exmouth-street and Coppice-row; down the little court by the side of the workhouse; across the classic ground which once bore the name of Hockley-in-the-hole; thence into Little Saffron-hill; and so into Saffron-hill the Great: along which the Dodger scudded at a rapid pace, directing Oliver to follow close at his heels. (Dickens [1837–8], Horne, 2003: 63)

This route can be easily mapped onto Booth (see Figure 20). The Booth map is made sixty years later than *Oliver Twist*, but many of the sites of poverty and criminality have a long history and so remain the same over time. The workhouse mentioned in the text corresponds to the Clerkenwell workhouse. Below this is the 'classic ground which once bore the name of Hockley-in-the-hole'

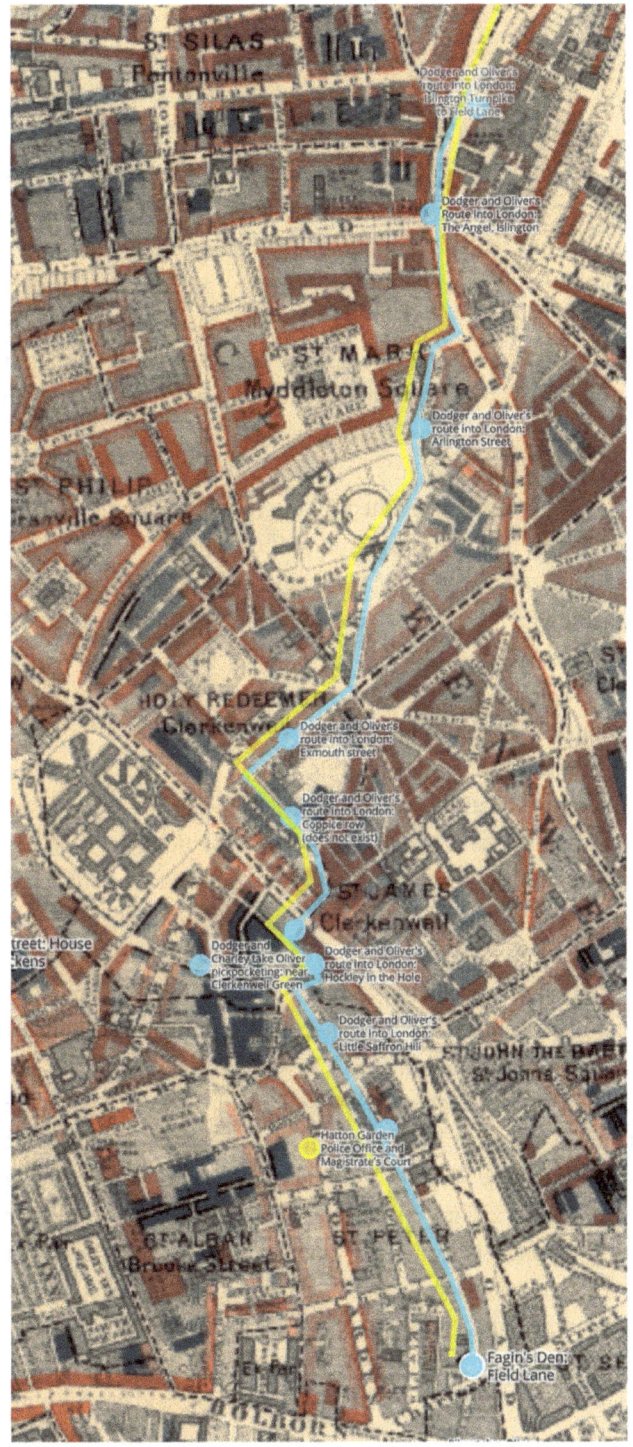

Figure 20 Route into London of Dodger (turquoise) and Oliver (yellow) mapped onto Charles Booth *Map of London Poverty, 1898–9*. In public domain.

(63) – a reference to a notorious part of the city in the eighteenth century, frequented by thieves and highwaymen.

When we look at where the two boys move we can see that they avoid main roads and, as they get closer to their destination, start to skirt along the edge of areas of extreme poverty (marked in blue, dark blue, and black) staying in close proximity, but not moving through them directly. After a strongly correspondent sense of the route in the first paragraph above, in the next the language becomes more indirect to give a generic sense of the claustrophobic nature of such spaces – describing 'covered ways and yards' and 'little knots of houses' (63) inhabited by threatening figures.[23]

The boys' destination – Fagin's first den – is located on the edge of a wealthy street in a kind of hinterland created by the railways and the markets, but with narrow slum streets and courts all around it (see Figure 21). The bottom of the road marked 'Great Saffron Hill' was previously called 'Field Lane' and was famous for selling handkerchiefs pickpocketed from the rich (Dickens [1837–8], Horne, 2003: n.8, 495–96).

On the Booth map a black square is conveniently marked at this point (perhaps because of this).[24] We chose to locate Fagin's 'house near Field-lane' here (Dickens [1837–8], Horne, 2003: 63). This area is perfect for Fagin. To the left is Hatton Garden, home to those in the jewellery trade. To the right is Smithfield market. In his Police Notebook for this beat, Booth's assistant, George Duckworth, notes: '"used to be a night patrol here but there is none now". Dampier [the policeman] thinks there still ought to be because of the value of the property' (B353, 251). So the placement of Fagin's hideout is extremely well chosen in terms of nesting the fictional within the real. This allows actual/historical and fictional spaces to interfuse in the mind of the reader in just the kinds of way Bakhtin desires.

It is notable that (with the exception of Bill Sikes's Chertsey Expedition) everyone tends to enter and leave London the same way, creating a strong North–South axis on the map (see Figure 22). This is because of Dickens's fondness for the Great North Road – a core chronotope running, as we can see, literally and metaphorically through *Oliver Twist*. This ancient highway linked England and Scotland and was a major stagecoach route in the nineteenth century. The traditional starting point for the Great North Road was Smithfield Market from which it led up to Angel, Islington (a key staging post), with the exit point for the city to the East of Highgate then out to Barnet and Hatfield. Although the road itself is only mentioned

---

[23] This region also corresponds to an area in easy proximity to Dickens's own house in Doughty Street where he lived while writing the book.

[24] Frustratingly, this is just beyond the edge of the police walk recorded in the notebook so the rationale for the black colour coding (semi-criminal) is not given.

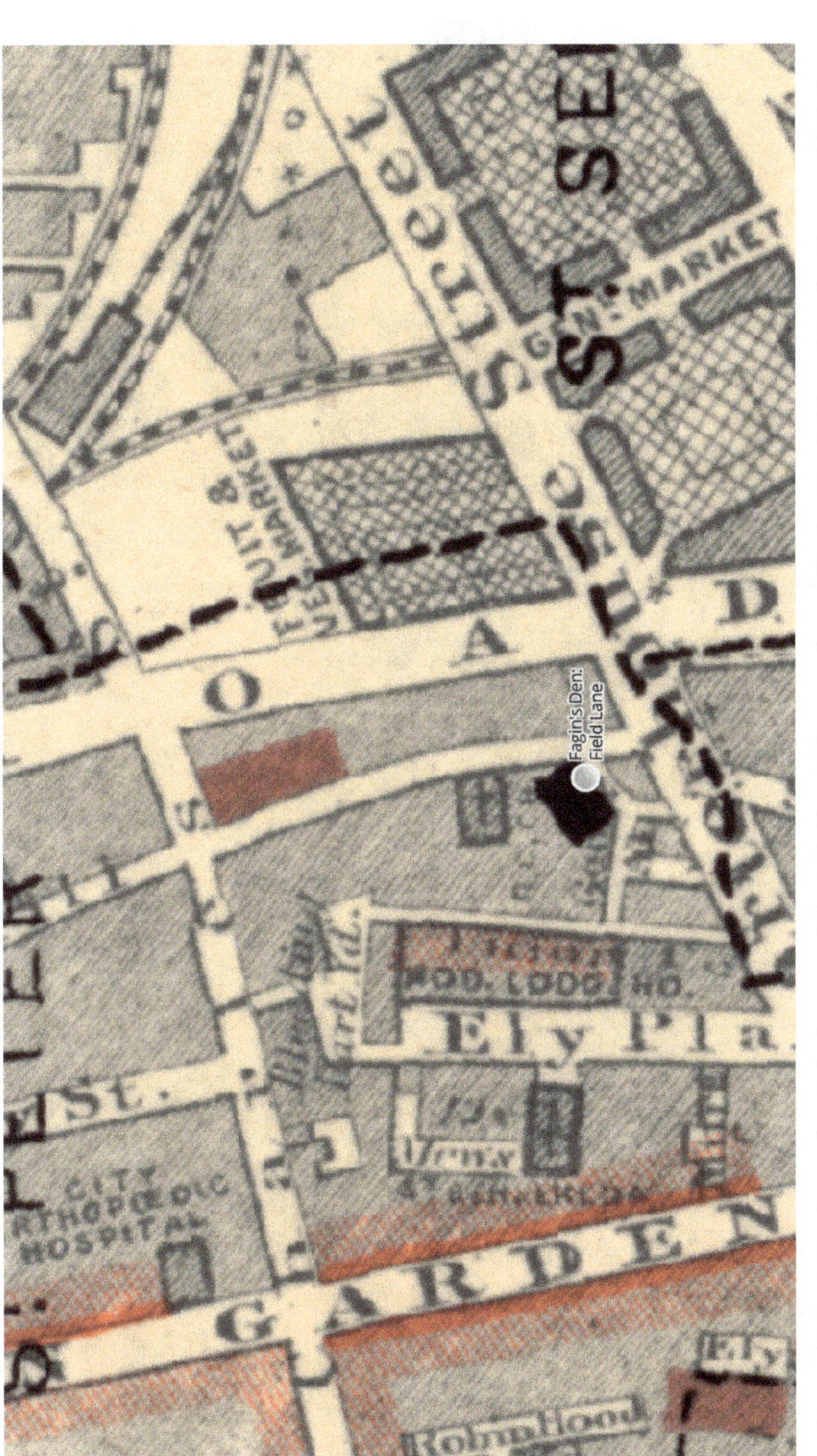

Figure 21 Fagin's primary den at the bottom of Great Saffron Hill mapped onto Charles Booth *Map of London Poverty*, 1898–9. In public domain.

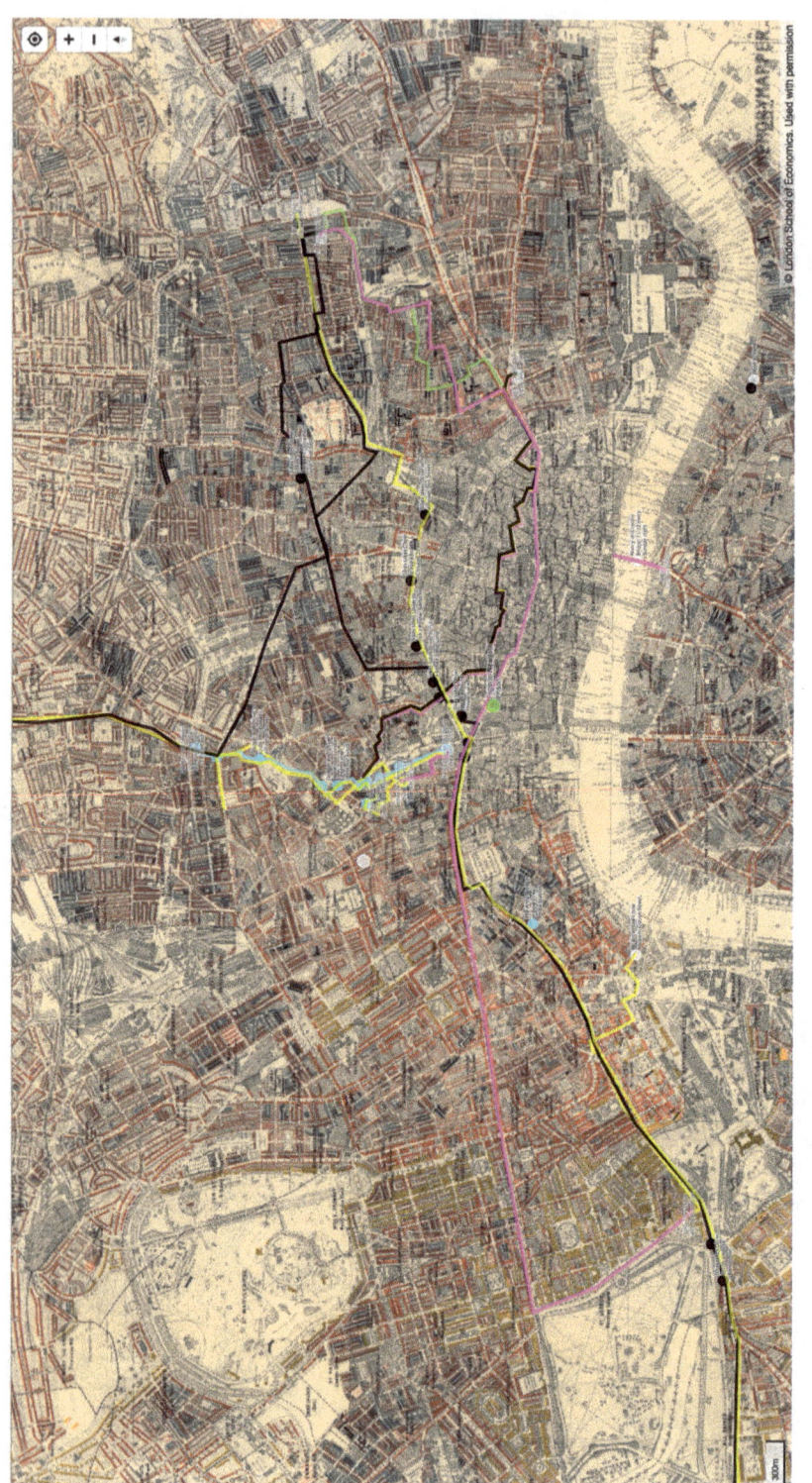

Figure 22 Central London of *Oliver Twist* mapped onto Charles Booth *Map of London Poverty* 1898–9. In public domain.

directly once in the text, this is the route taken *into* London by Oliver, Dodger, and others, and then the same route is followed *out* of London by Sikes on his wild wander after murdering Nancy.[25] As Oliver's starting point is a fictional place this could have been located anywhere relative to the capital. Dickens thus seems to want to *deliberately* draw attention to the North–South route and create repeated travel of different kinds by different characters over the same ground.

Another characteristic of Dickens's realism that is illuminated by mapping the text onto historic London is the double level of spatial indeterminacy at both a representational and referential level. For example, Fagin's boys move in a distinctive way through the city: 'It was not until the two boys had scoured with great rapidity through a most intricate maze of narrow streets and courts, that they ventured to halt ... beneath a low and dark archway' (Dickens [1837–8], Horne, 2003: 95). As this suggests, their routes are rarely mappable since they suddenly appear and disappear at will, making use of the spatial complexity of the slums. In *Capital Offences*, Simon Joyce suggests that Dickens's method of blurring the known and indistinct (the 'reality effect') served a distancing purpose:

> [B]y providing a kind of reality effect in his depictions of the urban underworld, Dickens generated a sense of trust in reforming and conservative readers alike, thereby assenting to the iconic reputation of Dickens as the prevailing chronicler and interpreter of lower-class London. (Joyce, 2003: 65)

Yet it is also the case that the nature of spatial representation matches the realist strategies of the text. That is to say, the deliberately untraceable nature of criminal activity justifies the indirect representation of place and space. In a similar way, because the narrative is often concerned with tracking Oliver and hunting him down (in case he tells others where the dens are located), non-specific directions given to characters in the story replicate the effects of realism on the reader. So, when Nancy goes to the police station to try and collect Oliver she is told only that he has been taken to 'somewhere at Pentonville' (Dickens [1837–8], Horne, 2003: 103) and her trail goes cold.

All of the criminal characters always travel at great speed. However, mapping onto a historical layer uncovers varying spatialities. Mapping Fagin reveals that he is the most hidden and stationary of the main characters. This complicates James Buzard's claim that 'the antisocial characters of Dickens's imagination seem ceaselessly and unpredictably on the move, driven by some perpetual-motion machine' (Buzard, 2005: 126). Fagin's initial stasis may well speak of his centrality and power in the criminal gang: other characters and actions orbit around him. His positioning ranges from the Field Lane/Saffron Hill area at his first appearance,

---

[25] At the start of Chapter 42, Noah Claypole and Charlotte also explicitly advance 'towards London, by the Great North Road' (Dickens, 1837–8; Horne, 2003: 348).

through Whitechapel, Bethnal Green to Jacob's Island, and, finally, Newgate (see Figure 23). However, his exact start and end points are never given.

Like Oliver, Nancy is mobile, but circumscribed. For the majority of the novel her movements are at others' bidding and, like the other criminal characters, Nancy moves in a wilfully resistant manner. For instance, after her unsuccessful attempt to collect Oliver from the police station Nancy returns, 'by the most devious and complicated route she could think of, to the domicile of the Jew' (Dickens [1837–8], Horne, 2003: 103). This represents a challenge to mapping: how can we be faithful to the text when routes are so deliberately slippery? Far from knowing which way Nancy takes here, all we know is the route she *does not* take – the direct one.

Such questions return us to strategies employed by the *Literary Atlas of Europe* project. In Section 1 we touched upon the mapping of routes by Reuschel et al. (2009: 9) and their solution for non-specific places in literature in terms of defining three levels of certainty:

> Direct: 'taken from the text'
> Indirect: 'plausible'
> Implied: 'interpreted'.

Whilst this is helpful, in any attempt to map a realist novel it rapidly becomes clear that there are actually two different kinds of spatial uncertainty conflated in these categories. One concerns perceived 'accuracy' in terms of correspondence to named locations on the earth's surface; the other concerns continuity between fictional and correspondent space. Thus, we need to distinguish between the following:

1. A varying degree of referential correspondence to the geo-spatial

- Direct correspondence to well-known place names at fixed sites ('The Angel, Islington')
- Direct, but not exact, place name correspondence ('a street in Pentonville')
- Direct, but generic/for an area ('Whitechapel')
- Direct, but fictional[26]
- Fictional and indirect/not named (Fagin's old den).

---

[26] Notably, Dickens does not employ this category in *Oliver Twist*. Apart from the starting point in rural 'Mudfog' and the indeterminate location of 'The Three Cripples' pub on Saffron Hill, he either uses existing place names – although often at a street level – or does not name and place specifically at all (Bill's house; Fagin's old den). All references are to the Penguin edition (Dickens, 1837–8; Horne, 2002), which has very detailed spatial information that informed the maps as well.

Figure 23 Fagin's movements mapped onto 'Society for the Diffusion of Useful Knowledge' (SDUK) map, 1836. In public domain from Wikimedia Commons.

2. *A varying degree of spatial continuity in representation of movement over time*

- Movement described in detail from street to street with one clear route [direct; no optionality]
- Movement described using clear waypoints along a defined route [direct; some optionality]
- Movement described with place names at considerable distance from each other [direct; considerable optionality]
- Movement not described at all, but the character must have travelled there [implicit; full optionality].

Nancy's movements vary considerably both in terms of referential correspondence and spatial continuity. Later in the novel, her independent movements (to the West End, to London Bridge) are increasingly punctuated by waypoints along a route. Where Oliver's journey into London from the Angel Islington to Field Lane is tightly mapped (see Figure 20), Nancy's route from East to West London, though much further in distance, is recounted in a few paragraphs. Having arrived at the West End Hotel and secured a meeting with Rose Maylie, Nancy promises to make herself visible, 'Every Sunday night, from eleven until the clock strikes twelve ... I will walk on London Bridge if I am alive' (Dickens [1837–8], Horne, 2003: 337). This is a classic Bakhtinian chronotope at the heart of the plot – the arranged meeting – an absolutely specific time and place knotted within it that also connects across real and represented layers as a kind of 'hotspot'. The motif of meeting is 'part of the concrete chronotope that subsumes it' and, as such, takes on 'different nuances' (Bakhtin, [1937] 1984: 97). Within a macro-chronotope of Victorian crime, where every criminal character's spatiality is characterised by rapid unseen movement, waiting at a fixed and public point with no easy hiding places nearby is the one thing a character should never do.

Nancy's desperation to stick to these meetings rouses Fagin's suspicions and he commissions a spy to trace her movements. As a result, the beginning of her final journey to meet Maylie and Brownlow is accurately narrated because it is observed and reported by Noah Claypole as he tracks her: 'To the left ... take the left hand, and keep on the other side' (Dickens [1837–8], Horne, 2003: 379). However, as the passage continues, the narrative recounts only what Claypole observes; there is no need for him to pay attention to the route taken since his orders are to report back the place Nancy arrives *at*, not *how* she arrives there. When she achieves her destination at the very start of the next chapter, direct correspondence returns, as an omniscient narrator looks down on them *both* from above: 'The church clocks chimed three quarters past eleven as two figures emerged on London Bridge ... they crossed the bridge, from the Middlesex to the Surrey shore' (380).

The nature of the narrative shifts that occur in relating her journey make it a challenge to map despite the fact that it is highly purposeful twice over (and extremely significant to the plot). So perhaps the only way to visualise this is via gaps and certainties in the text (Figure 24). It is not simply the case that Nancy moves through unspecified areas on her way to London Bridge, she literally disappears from the reader's view (while implicitly remaining entirely in the sight of Claypole). This is significant, because when Dickens makes use of the chapter break to have Nancy re-emerge at the Bridge at the start of the next chapter, she emerges referentially, representationally, and chronotopically. Her location is known and named, out in the open, just as her betrayal is exposed and her fate doomed.

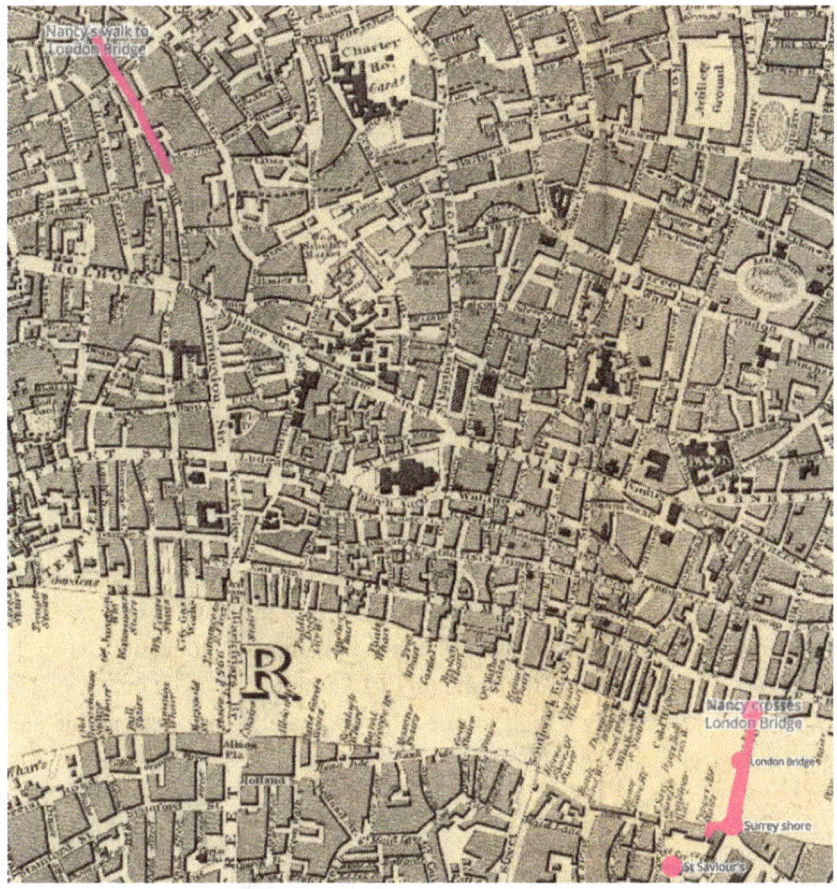

Figure 24 Start and end of Nancy's route from Little Saffron Hill to London Bridge on SDUK map.

Bill Sikes's spatiality is very different from that of the others, even though they all journey through the same back alleys and side streets. For one thing, his movement is marked by extreme caution: a dog runs on ahead to warn him, and even when they arrive at a safe house, he does not enter directly, but observes from a distance first. His hideout is never located specifically. Sikes also covers by far the greatest distance and goes approximately 25 miles off the map of central London in two directions, as the visualisation makes explicit (Figure 26). In describing his journeys Dickens uses the same technique as for Nancy, though on a larger scale, with distances between known sites extending further as he moves out into the country.

The first journey is from Bethnal Green to Chertsey (see Figure 25). This is highly purposeful goal-directed travel, with a known end point and objective, following an East–West trajectory. At first the route is even more tightly mapped than Oliver's into London:

> Turning down Sun-street and Crown-street, and crossing Finsbury square, Mr Sikes struck, by way of Chiswell-street, into Barbican, thence into Long-lane, and so into Smithfield. (Dickens [1837–8], Horne, 2003: 171)

The route is completely unambiguous. The listing of place names performs the movement of the text, speeding the tempo of the prose as the two move rapidly through the streets. There is no sense of Sikes avoiding the main streets or taking a devious path. Smithfield, a well-known landmark and the locus towards which everything in the preceding paragraphs has been working (the commercial centre), acts as a beacon to help ground the route in the reader's imagination. The clock of St Andrew's church, 'hard upon seven' (Dickens [1837–8], Horne, 2003: 172), fixes the journey in time and space – but only momentarily as it hurries Sikes on.

But the map can only go *so far* in drawing this out. It cannot, for instance, show how long the narrative pauses in Smithfield. The two lines (yellow and black) indicate that there are two walkers: Oliver in yellow, Sikes in black. But what the passage is doing, that the map is not able to do, is *alternating between* the two perspectives. Sikes, object-driven, 'bestowed very little attention on the numerous sights and sounds, which so astonished the boy' (171–2); Oliver, knowing neither route nor destination and being dragged along, notices all the sights and sounds, and it is through him that Smithfield is dwelt on.

The second of Sikes's long journeys is the novel's only instance of non-directed travel:

> He went through Islington; strode up the hill at Highgate ... turned down to Highgate Hill, unsteady of purpose, and uncertain where to go; struck off to the right again, almost as soon as he began to descend it; and taking the foot-path across the fields, skirted Caen Wood, and so came on Hampstead Heath. (Dickens [1837–8], Horne, 2003: 398)

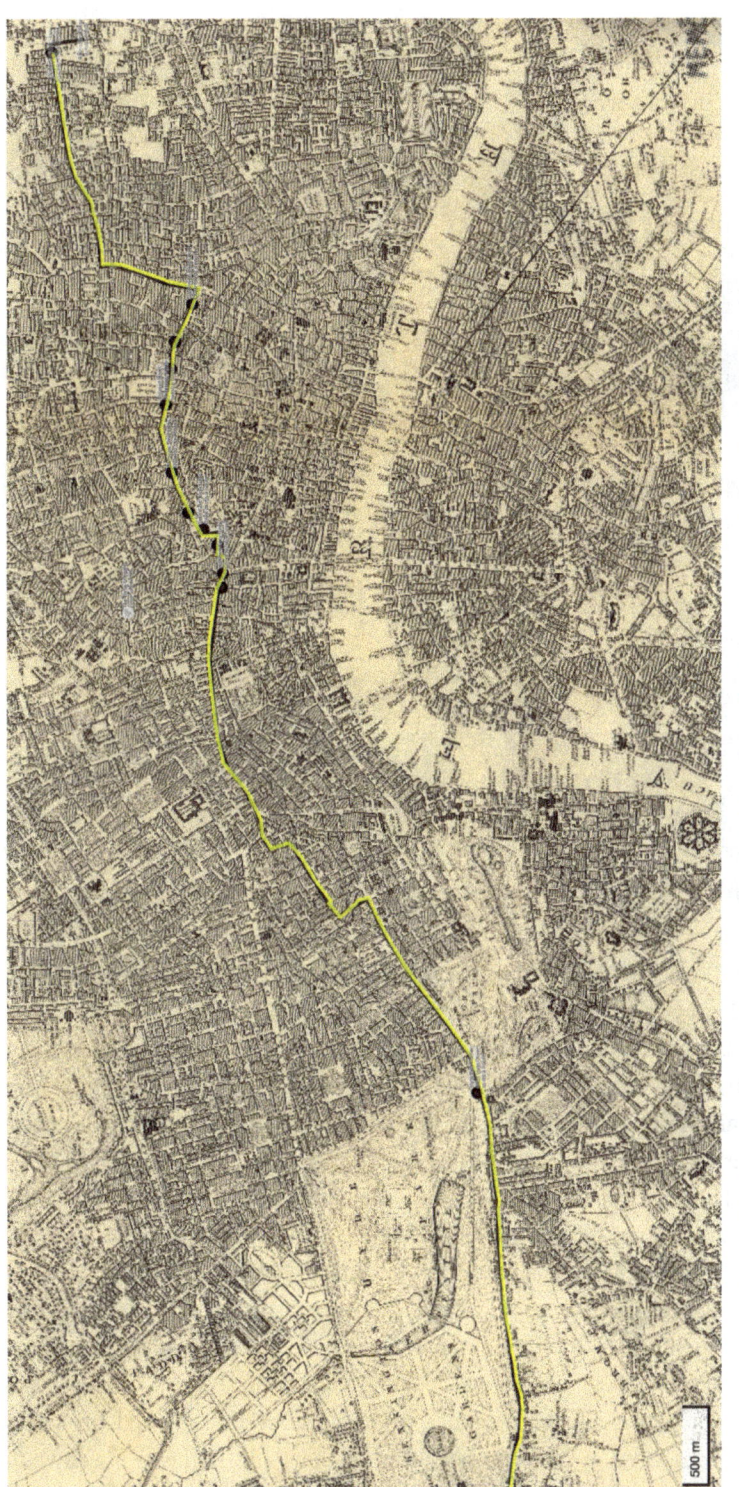

Figure 25 Bill Sikes and Oliver's route out of London (Bethnal Green to Hyde Park) on SDUK map.

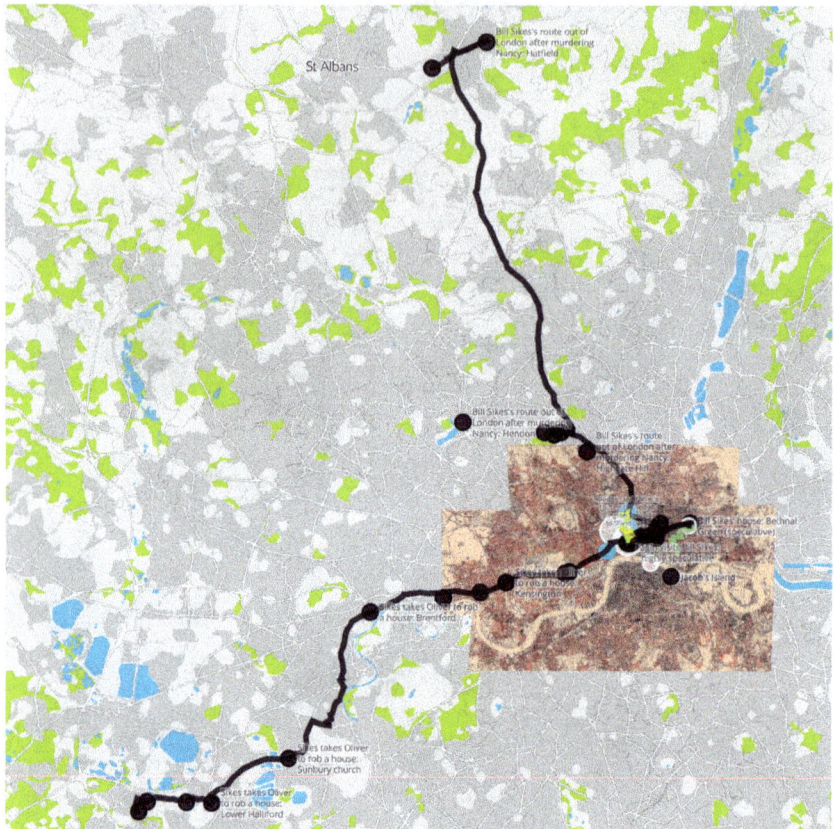

Figure 26 Bill Sikes's routes out of London beyond the Booth map.

The reverse trajectory (south to north) spatialises the inversion of purpose: flight. The map (Figure 26) reveals that, as with Sikes's earlier journey out, the further he travels from London, the further the distance between the waymarks. In contrast to the street-by-street account of the earlier journey from Shoreditch to Holborn, here the points are more inexact. There is no sense, for instance, of exactly *which* streets Sikes takes as he passes 'through Islington', only that he is heading towards Highgate. The Chertsey 'Expedition' has Sikes almost oblivious to his surroundings, focussing instead on moving forward and as quickly as possible. In contrast, here, Sikes is continually distracted by uncertainty of direction. The passage alternates between decisiveness ('strode off' and 'struck off') and passivity ('almost as soon as', 'skirted', and 'came upon'). The circularity and repetition that characterises Sikes' wandering ('again', 'wandering up and down', and 'already traversed') is also enacted at a formal level. The to-ing and fro-ing of movement is mirrored in the almost chiastic 'up the hill at Highgate ... down to

Highgate Hill'. Thus, the loosely mapped route, appearing as a long, northerly path but with numerous looped offshoots, spatially symbolises Sikes's self-traumatised state.

Finally, Sikes's longest journey exemplifies another of the novel's core spatial strategies: the route *out* is narrated in detail but the return journey is left almost entirely implied. This is the case, too, with the return from Chertsey for Sikes, from the West End Hotel for Nancy and from London Bridge (for both Nancy and Claypole). We are told that Sikes 'resolved to lie concealed within a short distance of the metropolis, and, entering it at dusk by a circuitous route, to proceed straight to that part of it which he had fixed on for his destination' (Dickens [1837–8], Horne, 2003: 406). The narrative technique makes it appear, by a shift in tense ('entering it at dusk'), as though this is narrated in real time, but this is only what Sikes *plans* to do – we have no idea if it is enacted in this way, since the journey is not narrated. This is a key challenge to real-world mapping: how can we map movement that occurs 'offstage' and in a way that acknowledges and does justice to such moments of deliberate verbal evasion? In such examples we can see how even works of high realism resist the attempt to be fixed absolutely. In short, *Oliver Twist* exceeds the map.

Releasing the Referential: *Oliver Twist*

Perhaps, then, we should turn to an alternative means of authentically mapping literary place and space by generating visualisations directly from the text, using the novel itself as the base map. This involves a reconceptualising of what it means to 'map' literature in terms of internal dynamics. Using graph network visualisations from the *Chronotopic Cartographies* project we wish to conclude Section 2 by analysing *relative* rather than *absolute* maps of literary time-space within the text; freeing ourselves from the problems of referentiality since the graph topology generated is a direct visualisation of the text itself.

At the start of our analysis of mapping realism we noted that the realist novel was suited to chronotopic mapping for two reasons: because of its concretisation of actual/fictional sites in space and time and because of chronotopic proliferation. Bakhtin makes it clear that 'a single work [might contain] a number of different chronotopes and complex interactions ... it is common moreover for one of these chronotopes to envelop or dominate the others' (Bakhtin, [1937] 1984: 252). The core of Bakhtin's argument is that *each* text contains a network of genres and chronotopes, some inherited, some contemporaneous, and some emerging.

This is certainly true of *Oliver Twist* in which the macro-chronotopic identity – criminal nineteenth-century London – also contains the multiple generic spaces of melodrama performed in the chronotopic sites of 'parlour' and 'public square': the Newgate novel ('public square' and 'castle'), detective fiction ('encounter' and 'threshold)', the picaresque novel ('encounter' and 'the road'), and the *Bildungsroman* ('the road'). In this way, it upends the sense that certain events occur in certain settings to generate genre, since the mosaic of urban realism contains multiple genres and chronotopes within it.

One fundamental way that realism achieves its effect is by *nesting* fictional spaces within a network of correspondent places or in proximity and juxtaposition to a well-known city. In a sense then, realism itself functions spatially in terms of a metonymic relationship that the spatial network brings to light. The whole – a network of real place naming with corresponding sites in the world – creates an illusion of totality for the fictional part nestled within it. For example, Jane Austen's Northanger Abbey is a destination in Gloucestershire reached by a long carriage journey from the city of Bath. Since the first half of the book is set in this well-known Regency resort, with frequent accurate street and place naming ('Pulteney Street', 'Milsom Street', and 'the Pump Room'), the fact that the move into the country is also a move to an entirely fictional location with no correspondence of any kind is easily overlooked.

George Gissing also uses the nested device for *New Grub Street* (1891), a realist novel that takes realism itself as its theme and functions in a way comparable to *Oliver Twist*. It begins in Wattleborough, a fictional village but one which, situated on the Great Western line, is in part characterised by its proximity to London. (In a similar way, *Oliver Twist* starts out in a fictional village and then follows the Great North Road into London.) For Gissing, once in London, 'New Grub Street' itself is also fictional, situated in Cripplegate but referring back to an earlier eighteenth-century Grub Street (renamed Milton street in 1830) famous for hack writers. Here realism is both spatially and temporally contained.

The nested nature of realism has two consequences for the mapping of such texts. First it lends itself to a multiple chronotopic model with fictional spaces contained within larger pockets of accurate correspondent place naming. Second, this problematises any direct mapping of the text onto actual geolocations because core fictional sites do not have *any* correspondence and can only be mapped relatively (not absolutely) to real world sites.

Oliver Twist exemplifies the realist use of nesting. In fact, Oliver himself is a kind of cuckoo repeatedly being thrown out of one nest and into another. This occurs both in his fictional place of origin and once he gets to London with the negative fictional sites of Fagin's dens, Sikes's rooms, and the Three Cripples

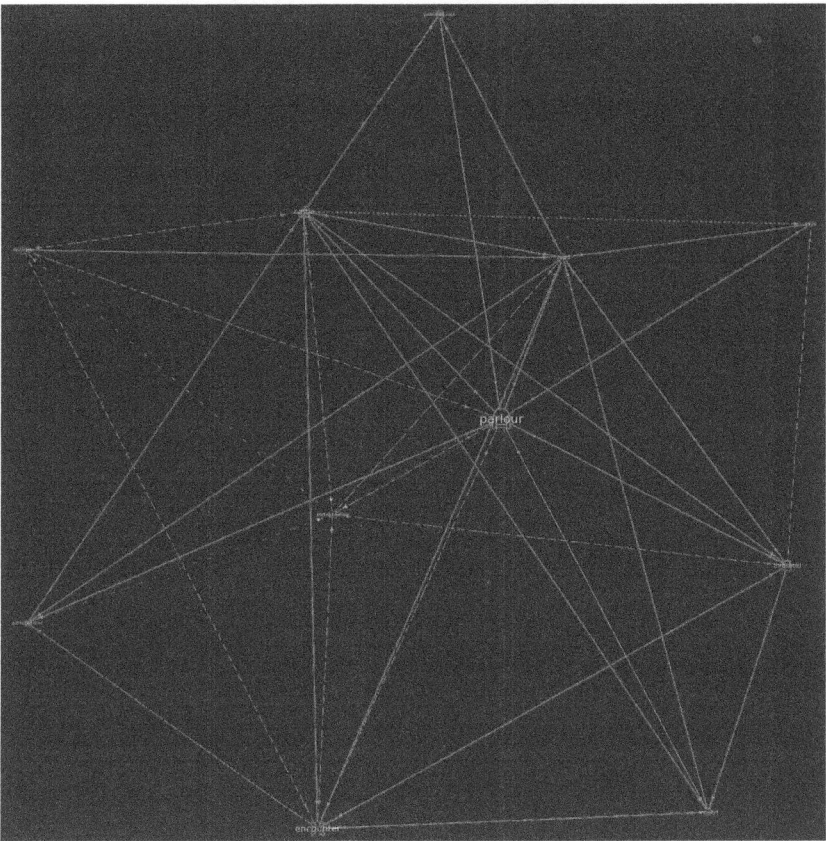

Figure 27 Deep Chronotope map for *Oliver Twist*.

pub; and the positive ones of Mr Brownlow's and the Maylies's houses. This is why when we look at the Deep Chronotope map (Figure 27) the most dominant chronotope for the novel and one that connects many of the others is the interior space of the 'parlour'. This is entirely counter to the impression received from mapping referentially where internal sites were often not locatable on the map and where routes and movements strongly predominated – drawing attention to the chronotopes of the 'road' and 'encounter' (which *are* also highly significant, as discussed in the previous section).

If we turn to the Complete map of *Oliver Twist* (Figure 28), we see, then, that it aligns with the realist strategy itself; visualising the conceived world as a totality but one that contains many nested sub-spaces within it. This map visualises every coded aspect of the text. It displays the topoi and their chronotopic values (these are the graph nodes), the toporefs or secondary named places (within the nodes), and the connections between them (edges or lines).

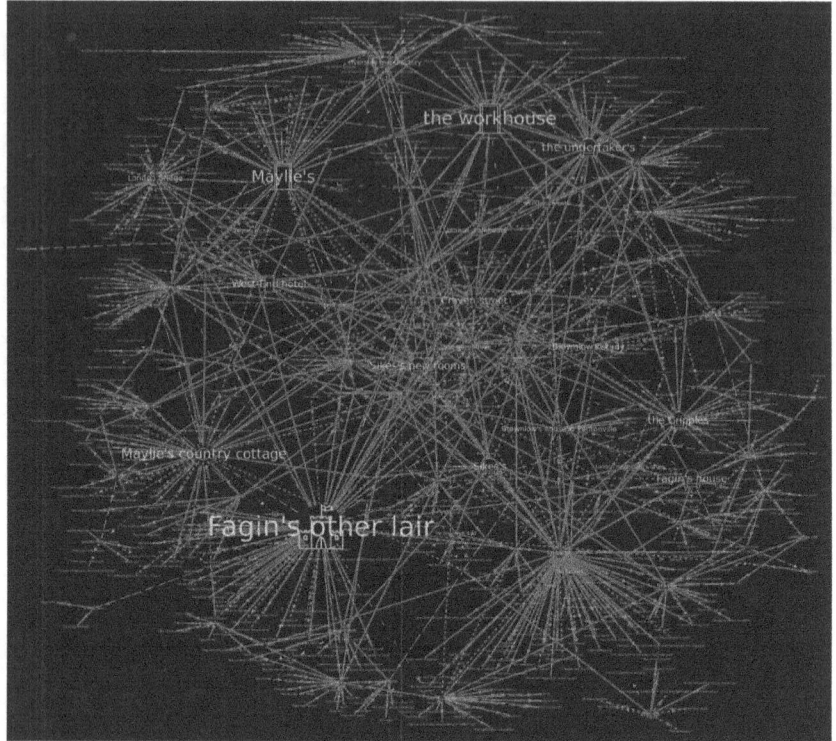

Figure 28 Complete map for *Oliver Twist*.

The chronotopic method gives every kind of place – referential, indirect, and fictional – equal prominence. As a result, it partially addresses the problem of visualising realism as identified by Tambling, who contends that Dickens's London is 'a place of multiple connections which baffles representation or "cognitive mapping"' (Tambling, 2012: 16). At the same time its complexity is so high that it is virtually unreadable (the map that contains everything is not a good map).

Luckily however, a chronotopic method generates a map series that prioritises the same spatial information in different ways and with the ability to generate sub-maps or nested maps by only visualising a section of the text (for different characters, narrative voices, sections of a narrative, and sub-generic spatial forms). Where the graph topology of the Complete map presents a complex totality at a small scale that limits it accordingly, by mapping *parts* of that whole separately, larger-scale embedded maps can be generated that tell us a lot more about a particular aspect of the text's spatial, narrative, or chronotopic value. In the case of *Oliver Twist* micro-mapping can draw out the spatial details and characteristics of the chronotope of crime, a closed network of unstable and fluid sites. The chronotope of crime is defined by Bakhtin as the "'social exotic" – "slums", "dregs", the world of thieves' which sits within 'familiar territory' (Bakhtin, [1937] 1984: 245). As we shall see, mapping *Oliver Twist* demonstrates the centrality of this chronotope and that it is just as spatially realised as the surface-level realism.

Where the layering of text onto a historical map emphasised bearings and routes, the chronotopic map provides the kind of multi-scalar model desired in Section 1. The first thing it draws attention to is the relative prominence of the novel's key nested spaces: Fagin's other ken (hideout) in Whitechapel, Rose Maylie's house near Chertsey, the workhouse, and the various other dens (Fagin's house, Sikes's, and Sikes's new rooms). Let's look in more detail at the largest of these, 'Fagin's other lair' – with this part of the text coded separately to produce a secondary map. On the real-world map this location 'baffles representation' because it falls into the category hardest to pin down: unnamed and fictional. The text deliberately doesn't locate the 'other ken' as part of its realism effect.

Figure 29 is a micro-map of just this section of the text and the sub-naming within it. The first thing to notice is the approach to it via the indistinctly labelled 'London Streets'. Here, then, is Bakhtin's 'social exotic' with direct references (shown with solid lines) to 'little frequented and dirty ways' and a 'filthy narrow street'. The indirect connections (dashed double lines) to 'Bartlemy' and 'the thundering old jail' are in a coded language in line with the camouflaged setting. After the unnamed streets, the lair itself, accessible only via 'the passage', 'a flight of stairs', 'an empty kitchen', and 'a small back yard', is a nested and clandestine space. It can be looked out from (via 'Oliver's observatory') but not into. After all, a lair can only be a lair if it is secret. Here, indirect references to 'the house of correction' and 'the Old Bailey' also set the den in opposition to spaces of authority. What the micro-map neatly visualises is the two means by which the nested spaces of crime are entered and exited: through wilfully disguised streets or via narrative movements (dashed lines). The map also displays the *narrative* proximity of Fagin's den to the other spaces of Oliver's dwellings – the workhouse, Brownlow's – which appear at the top of the map. By implication, though, the narrative jump also implies physical detachment (and thus a tension between narrative, geographic, and subjective experiences as well as between respectable London and its dirty, unseen side).

The method of correspondent mapping, which relies on the specificity of the real-world map via place names, emphasises a sense of control and order which only tells half the story when it comes to the spatial identity of *Oliver Twist*. In so doing, it constructs a false hierarchy which values mappable over fictional places. Mapping chronotopically therefore draws out a tension at the heart of the

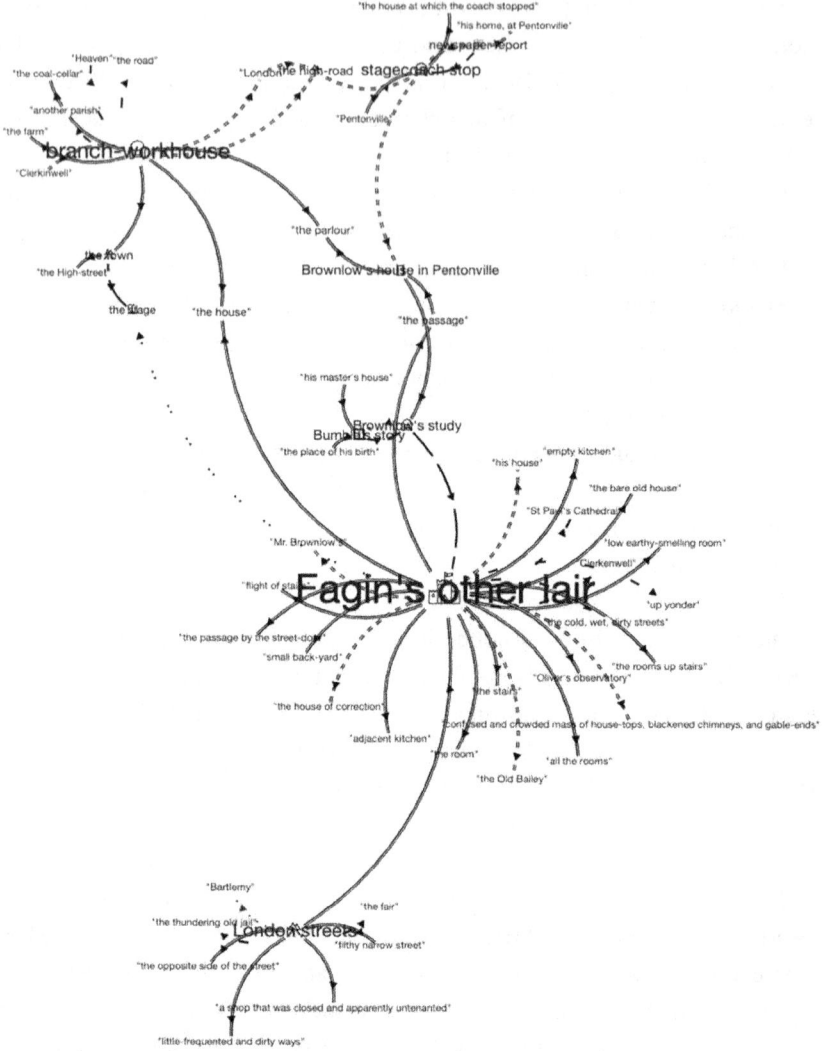

Figure 29 Secondary Chronotope map for Fagin's Den.

text. On the one hand, the known locations, real place names, and scrupulous attention to urban topography create what Peter Brown defines as 'simulacra'. In this mode, literary descriptions mimic the 'real' to produce 'the thrill of recognition [as] part of the text's appeal' (Brown, 2006: 18). However, counter to this runs an alternative geography in a network of alleyways and courts whose very nature is to resist discovery and, therefore, mapping. We mapped Dickens onto Booth to show how named sites in the text corresponded to areas of extreme poverty and social concern, which the author wants the work to explicitly address. But at the same time this is a work of fiction about a hidden world, one that repeatedly pulls its victims into it, out of sight of the respectable and safe and from the wide boulevards into the shady courts and backstreets. Only the chronotopic map can reveal this.

This tension between counter impulses plays out further in the most readable map in the series, the Topoi map (Figure 30), which privileges key locations in the text. The first thing to notice is the relative absence of named places here. Characters may *move through* referential places, but they come to rest in represented fictional sites (criminal dens, country houses, cottages, and workhouses). The Topoi map confirms and extends the centrality of Fagin and his lair as seen in the Complete map. The dominance of 'Fagin's other lair' (it is the largest, most central and most connected topos) in the spatial network of the Topoi upends the hierarchy and allows the alternative geography to be at once revealed and indirect. The sense of movement and activity that plays out so clearly in the process of real-world mapping is still partly captured on the Topoi map in the solid lines. Here we can trace the journeys out of London looping out from and around the centre. However, what the map also brings to light is that *Oliver Twist* is just as much a novel of imagined (dashed orange lines) as it is referential spaces (doubled purple lines of direct and indirect connections). As we have seen, these imagined spaces are nested in a wider network of London which corresponds directly to locatable sites. This spatial quality of nesting plays out in two senses: boundedness and confinement.

This is registered in the range of chronotopic identities which characterise the experience of space: 'the castle', 'the parlour', and 'the idyll'. To Oliver, boundedness means confinement. To criminal characters like Fagin and Sikes, for most of the novel boundedness equates to security; to be 'off the map' is to be safe from the authorities. The final trajectory towards a known location, starting at Hatfield and ending at Jacob's Island for Sikes, and Newgate for Fagin, is one that ends with a single fixed point at the end of a rope.

To conclude, the main finding from mapping *Oliver Twist* in two different ways (absolute and relative) is that these acts turn out to be highly complementary. Mapping onto the real allows us to grasp spatial syntax and patterns of movement across the city far more clearly than verbal description can achieve and works to reveal the scale of movement for different characters. Such an act also shows how chronotopic sites work to anchor the narrative to real-world geography by means of moments in space and time that are of key significance to events in the literary text. In contrast, Chronotopic Cartography works like a counter image to reveal those areas that resist easy depiction, uncovering the core time-spaces of the novel and the importance of interiors – both physical and psychological. These combined literary mapping activities, undertaken alongside analysis of the text, result in a rich and complex spatial interpretation.

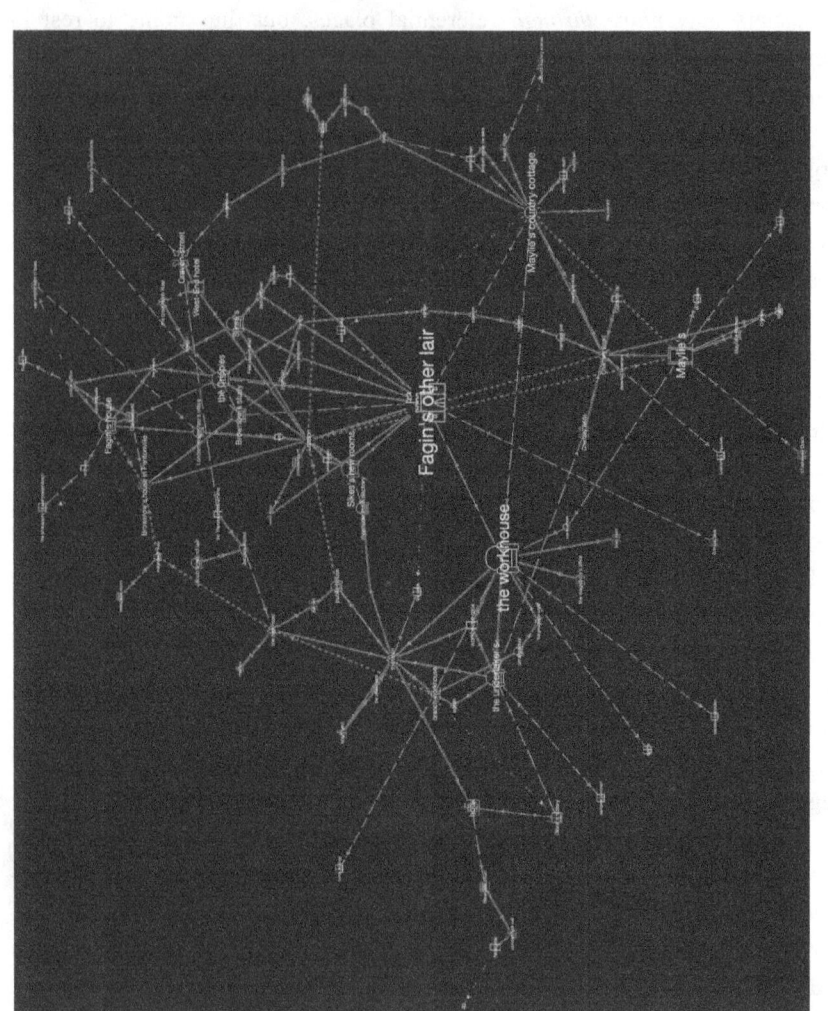

Figure 30 Topoi map for *Oliver Twist*.

3 Towards a Processual Mapping Method: Evolving Neverland

> [E]ither these are part of the island or they are another map showing through.
>
> (Barrie, [1911] 2019: 74)

The previous section explored the digital literary mapping of a realist novel comparatively by mapping onto historic map layers of Victorian London and by generating chronotopic maps out of the text itself. Mapping the same text in different ways provided complementary perspectives on literary place and space. In the final section of this Element we seek to develop and apply a processual interpretative method for digital literary mapping that respects the maps generated as open forms, 'knowledge generators' (Drucker, 2014: 135) in and through the example of J. M. Barrie's *Peter Pan* – a work of imaginative fantasy centred on a non-existent place. This work, which exists in five different textual states, is challenging in its chronotopic and generic uncertainty as well as in the complexity of spatial tensions it presents between realism and fantasy, for adult and child. Such a deeply unstable text allows us to map comparatively in a different way, across a textual totality, to explore a complex storied spatiality. As such it also tests and challenges the chronotopic mapping method by pushing it to its limits.

Since the mid-twentieth century the disciplines of Literary Studies and Cartography have been intertwined in a range of ways productive to both, informed by shared understanding of phenomenological accounts of 'being in the world' and the underpinning of spatial, social, and deconstructive theories that create common conceptual ground. In the field of Cartography, interpretation of maps has moved from a traditional view that maps represent objective information truthfully presented to a much more sceptical position by means of Critical Cartography (itself informed by literary theory). In the 'post-representational' approach that emerges from this, the map is not viewed primarily as a representation of place (coming after) but as an active creator of spaces: 'a map does not simply represent the world; it produces the world' (Kitchin et al., 2009: 17). When we respond to maps as spatial practices, this results in a major shift both in how maps are understood to work and the uses to which they are put. Above all, as Kitchin et al. make clear, this marks a shift from '*a* map' to 'mappings' (2009: 17). The resulting *processual approach* values maps as dynamic and fluid and focusses on what they *do* as much, or more, than what they represent. So,

> [m]aps rather are understood as always in a state of becoming; as always mapping; as simultaneously being produced *and* consumed, authored *and*

read, designed *and* used, serving as a representation *and* practice; as mutually constituting map/space in a dyadic relationship. (Kitchin et al., 2009: 17)

What is true in relation to the mapping of actual geography is also true for the mapping of *imaginary* geographies. In their exploration of a processual approach applied to the literary maps of Arthur Ransome, Cooper and Priestnall describe acts of mapping undertaken by the reader:

The reader is actively moving – in both physical and imaginative terms – between textual and cartographic representations of space in an attempt to understand the topology of Ransome's fictionalized place. (Cooper and Priestnall, 2011: 256)

Such an account provides an illuminating way to understand the nature of the interpretative method that underpins our digital mapping model for which the *critic* as map-maker 'shuttles back and forth between text and map, map and text' (2011: 256). A Bakhtinian model also allows for the possibility of exploring texts themselves as fluid, changing, spatio-temporal constructs that point up the dynamic nature of their meaning. The usefulness of such an approach in relation to digital literary mapping is clear. A processual method is inherently subjective and inherently dynamic, valuing the way in which forms and meanings change over time. The description of such acts of mapping as 'spatial practices enacted to solve relational problems' (Kitchin et al., 2012: 2) could stand as a definition of the work we seek to undertake here for literature.

Peter Pan as a Processual Text

In her influential critique of Children's Literature, *The Case of Peter Pan or The Impossibility of Children's Fiction*, Jacqueline Rose points out that 'J. M. Barrie's *Peter Pan* was retold before he had written it, and then rewritten after he had told it' (Rose, 1984: 67). Barrie repeatedly and publicly asserted a model of multiple co-authorship between himself and others, as well as between adult and child. As various critics remind us, at the first play's performance Barrie had the youngest member of the cast take the bow in place of himself as author.[27] Equally, in his dedication to the 1928 playscript for the five Llewellyn-Davies boys, to whom and with whom he first made up his stories, Barrie states:

I have no recollection of writing the play of *Peter Pan*. . . . You had played it until you tired of it, and tossed it in the air and gored it and left it derelict in the

---

[27] See Lancelyn Green, 1954; Jack, 1990; and Stirling, 2012.

mud and went on your way singing other songs; and then I stole back and sewed some of the gory fragments together with a pen-nib.

Any one of you five brothers has a better claim to the authorship than most, and I would not fight you for it ... 'To the Five: A Dedication'. (Barrie, [1928] 2019: 323, 326)[28]

Peter Pan then is a composite totality, one that seems to glory in its own multiplicity and the way in which it morphs across versions and forms over time.[29] The five main states are the following:

1902   Chapters 13–18 in *The Little White Bird* [One section within a book for adults]
1903–04   *Anon: a Play* performed but not published at the Duke of York's Theatre, London on 27th December[30]
1906   *Peter Pan in Kensington Gardens* [six chapters from *LWB* pub. separately][31]
1911   *Peter and Wendy* [prose narrative]
1928   *Peter Pan, or the Boy who would not grow up* [Play text revised and published].

Thus, it lends itself to a processual reading twice over. First, authorial habit tends towards repeated textual revision:

The idea that everything was capable of being changed into anything also lay at the heart of Barrie's habits as a writer. For in his eyes writing was a fluid process far more than it was a fixed product. (Douglas-Fairhurst, 2019: xxxi)

Similarly, Kirsten Stirling notes of Barrie that '[h]e plays with the question of origins throughout his play and his novel, and the very fact that his story exists in so many versions makes it difficult to establish what is the definitive text of *Peter Pan*' (Stirling, 2012: 3).

---

[28] All textual references except those for *Peter Pan in Kensington Gardens* are from Douglas-Fairhurst, 2019.
[29] This chapter focusses only on the main textual states. As Douglas Fairhurst puts it: 'The texts printed here reveal the main stages of this journey, but Barrie's itchy-fingered impulse to revise means that many interim versions survive in draft form. An edition that included every variant would run to several volumes' (xlvii). R. D. S. Jack identifies eleven 'origin versions' (Jack, 1990: 301).
[30] This play survives in two previously unpublished states: the 1903–04 manuscript held at the Lilly Library, University of Indiana, and the typed-up production text at Beinecke Library, Yale. See Jack, 1990, for comparison of these. The text quoted from and coded here is that of 1903–04 as reproduced in Douglas-Fairhurst, 2019.
[31] Peter Hollindale tells us that the differences between the chapters on Peter Pan in *Little White Bird* and *Peter Pan in Kensington Gardens* are 'slight' and he conveniently lists these (Hollindale, 1991: xxix-xxx). Hollindale's Oxford edition uses the later version as the base text; Douglas-Fairhurst's edition uses the earlier version.

Second, the figure of Peter is himself in process across texts, not subject to the same laws of time and growth over time that affect ordinary humans, and definitely unstable. This results in a deliberate and self-conscious denial of origins – the very characteristic that leads Rose to use *Peter Pan* as the case study in her powerful Freudian/Lacanian deconstructive attack on the entire concept of Children's Fiction. For her the textual totality is wilfully anti-teleological:

> The rest of Peter Pan's history can then be read as one long attempt to wipe out the residual signs of the disturbance out of which it was produced. The Little White Bird is an origin of sorts, but only in the sense that no origin is ever left behind, since it necessarily *persists*. (Rose, 1984: 5)

The effect is one of Lacanian disavowal on a large scale, permitting adult society to deny its own need, or reshape reality to meet that need through the construct of the idealised child:

> *Peter Pan*'s dispersion – the fact that it is everywhere and nowhere at one and the same time – has been taken as the sign of its cultural value. Its own ethereal nature merely sanctions the eternal youth and innocence of the child it portrays. (Rose, 1984: 6)

In this account, then, Peter himself is the lack that adult desire attempts (but fails) to fill over and over again, and repeated transformations of the text of *Peter Pan* attest to 'the difficulty of that process – the difficulty of the relation between adult and child' (Rose, 1984: 5). Proliferation is a sign of deeper underlying disturbance (authorial and cultural) that manifests itself in and through the mythification of Peter himself as the archetype of innocence (when he is anything but).

Peter Pan is relatively unusual in undertaking this evolution so publicly and across a range of forms. However, what happens when, rather than tracing a process textually (or *as well as* doing so), we spatialise or map it in multiple ways? Is what is true of the texts also true of the *spatiality* of those texts? This section will read the process of the *Peter Pan* totality by mapping it chronotopically, with a particular focus on exploring how the adult–child dynamic plays out in spatial terms. By exploring process both verbally *and* visually we hope to achieve a fuller sense of spatial meaning changing across the totality and explore the ways in which it may not matter that there is always 'another map showing through' (Barrie, [1911] 2019, 74).[32]

---

[32] Hollindale's note to this description states: 'It is essential to Barrie's vision that the geography of imagination is different for the child and the adult, but only for Peter Pan himself is childhood cartography unblemished by adult land-marks' (1991: 233).

Spatial Tensions in Kensington Gardens

It is time to return to the *Peter Pan* totality and put such ideas into practice by working across both maps and texts to undertake a comparative spatial reading that also explores a core concern for Children's Fiction – the way in which '[u]nder the surface of the children's book is a sharp and sometimes ferocious dialectic, exploring the collision and relation of the child and adult worlds' (Hollindale, 1991: xxi).

We can begin by comparing two very different maps for the earliest independent form of the text: *Peter Pan in Kensington Gardens*.[33] The map in Figure 31 is that made by Arthur Rackham for the first edition of 1906. As a literary map it immediately combines real and fictional spaces. It is a fairly accurate depiction of the real-world location with corresponding place names ('The Broad Walk', 'The Round Pond', and 'The Serpentine') but also

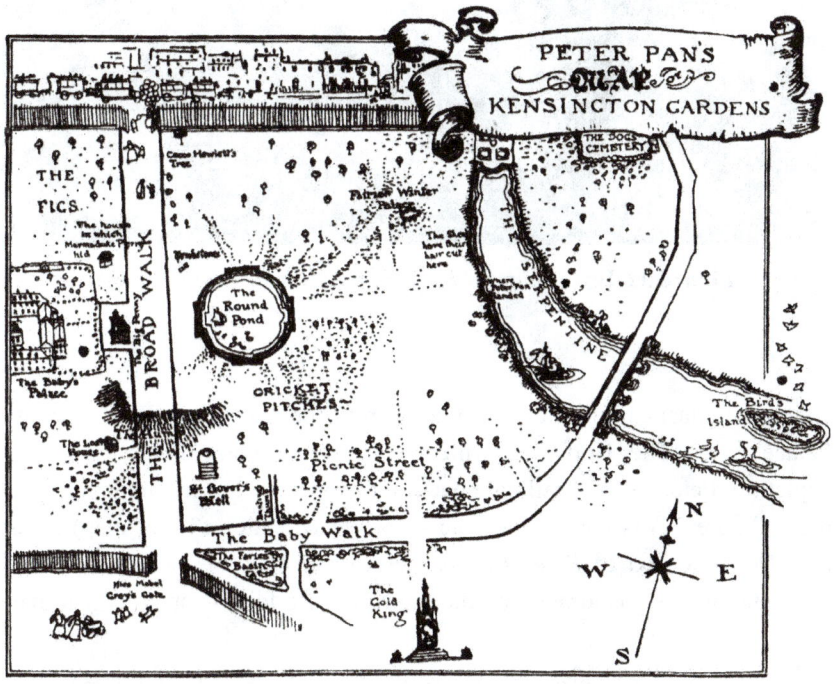

Figure 31 Arthur Rackham's map for *Peter Pan in Kensington Gardens*. Image from 1912 edition by Hodder and Stoughton. In public domain from Wikimedia Commons.

---

[33] The text quoted from here is the first edition version of 1906 (Hollindale, 1991).

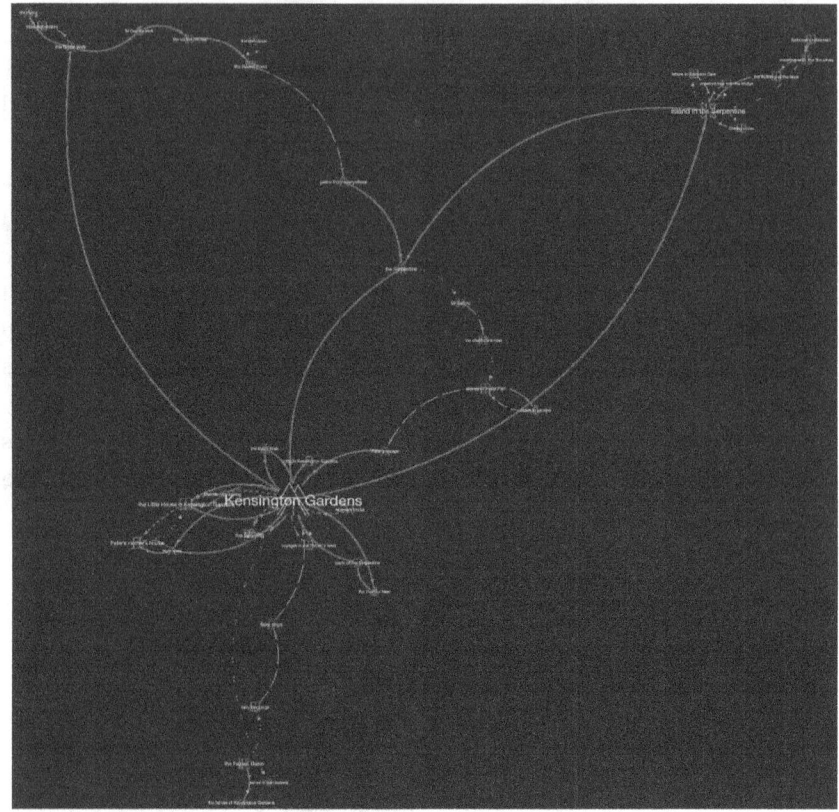

Figure 32 Topoi map for *Peter Pan in Kensington Gardens*.

contains fantastical and fictional places from the narrative ('Faeries Winter Palace' and 'The House in which Marmaduke Perry hid') as well as depicting Peter in his sailing boat on the river. The second map given here (Figure 32) is the chronotopic graph visualisation (Topoi map) generated from the text of *Peter Pan in Kensington Gardens*, which, appropriately enough, seems almost to take the form of a fairy – or at least to have wings.

The park that provides the setting for the first version of the text is an environment strongly, almost repressively, demarcated by the adults. In part this reflects the dominant mood and tone of the earlier full text of *The Little White Bird* (from which it is now detached), in which the adult narrator, somewhat disturbingly, undertakes 'manoeuvres to possess this child' (Hollindale, 1991: xix). Spatially, the effect is to emphasise external boundaries:

> The Gardens are bounded on one side by a never-ending line of omnibuses, over which your nurse has such authority that if she holds up her finger to any one of them it stops immediately. She then crosses with you in safety to the other side. There are more gates to the Gardens than one gate, but that is the one you go in at. (Barrie, [1906] 1991: 3)

The chronotopic identity of the Gardens is that of 'a safe space' controlled by protective adult figures. When we look at Rackham's map, the illustration emphasises this strong sense of boundedness, with fencing along top and bottom, and the main pathways and river setting internal limits. If we compare both of these with the digital map generated from the text (Figure 32, the Topoi map), we see that the dominant chronotopes are those of 'road' and 'encounter' within the park. Unsurprisingly, the same named locations are privileged – with 'The Broad Walk', 'The Round Pond' top left, and 'The Serpentine' in the middle. But the digital map strongly registers the discrete spaces of the fairies (bottom) and the island in the Serpentine as the habitation place of Peter Pan (top right). The distinction between adult and child now also correlates more strongly to that between geolocational/referential places able to be named and directly visited (connected in purple) and imaginary or fantastical ones (represented indirectly in orange).

What we find repeatedly in using topological maps to analyse spatial meaning is that they draw attention to a tension between different ways of experiencing and representing place and space that is latent in the text. Perhaps the most dominant form – a tension that is also a visual/verbal distinction – is that between 'map' and 'tour'. Here it is helpful to recall Michel de Certeau's comparison of these two spatial experiences in which the map functions as 'a plane projection totalizing observations' and the tour as 'a discursive series of operations' (de Certeau, 1980: 119). For de Certeau this distinction is part of a larger model of spatial power relations in which individual 'tactics' work against larger imposed 'strategies'. Where the map is concerned with 'seeing' and with a static geometric representation concerning the relative positioning of objects, the narrative style of the tour or itinerary is concerned with 'going'; with enabling the individual to negotiate that space from within. Each means of conceptualising space is, however, bound up with the other.

While both spatial practices are very much in play across *Peter Pan*, the distinction is complicated by its intersection with adult/child experiences and the way in which the former acts upon the latter. The first section of *Peter Pan in Kensington Gardens* is entitled 'The Grand Tour of the Gardens'. Here, the tour mode is so *emphatically* applied by the adult narrator that, rather than functioning in de Certeau's terms as a resistant discourse to the imposition and control of the map (the individual taking possession through spatial practices), it becomes a highly controlling trope for both the character and the reader. Narrative voice is strongly linked to containment of spatial experience for the child by the adult 'guide':

> You can't be good all the time at the Round Pond, however much you try. You can be good in the Broad Walk all the time, but not at the Round Pond, and the reason is that you forget, and, when you remember, you are so wet that you may as well be wetter. (Barrie, [1906] 1991: 7)

> Even though you had no intention of running you do run when you come to the Hump, it is such a fascinating slide-down kind of place. ([1906] 1991: 5)

The second person voice is so insistent that the actions and movements of the obedient child (David) seem almost predetermined by it. Thus, although both adult and child are technically on the 'tour', the adult voice functions far more like the totalising all-knowing perspective of the map. There is a division between the adult realist world (the safety of Kensington Gardens) and the imaginary playspace (being taken by fairies; Peter Pan). The former seeks to control the latter verbally and spatially, but cannot quite do so. In a larger sense perhaps this also points to the underlying impulses driving referential literary geography as opposed to Chronotopic Cartography – a desire to make places correspond to what is known, safe, familiar, as opposed to representing what is imagined or generated out of that place.

Space is cohabited but not really shared because the adult seeks to create an environment that is, above all, risk-free. The compliant child has a tightly constrained freedom within both place and text: 'multiply caught up in, possessed, and owned by the story' (Rose, 1984: 24). In terms of chronotopic identity there is a fine line between a positive space that allows for free play and pleasure (idyll) and the way in which this can morph into something more negative, controlling, and claustrophobic (castle).

With the appearance of Peter Pan, however, the figure of the child is doubled, as is the space itself, and a distance begins to open up. The sub-narrative for Peter is introduced as a shared imaginative endeavour between adult and child and this immediately releases it from the imposition of the second person voice:

> First I tell it to him, and then he tells it to me, the understanding being that it is quite a different story; and then I retell it with his additions, and so we go on until no one could say whether it is more his story or mine. . . . Well, Peter Pan got out by the window. (Barrie, [1906] 1991: 13)

In narrative terms, Peter is immediately much freer than David (from whose imagination he partly springs) and this is registered spatially as the civilised and surveillant adult world is now revealed to be the park of the *day* time. The second space is that of the night when the Gardens turn wild and inhuman. The temporal and physical boundary between these is marked by the Closing and Opening of the Gates and by 'Lock-out Time'. Place itself is literally turned inside out and Peter's situation is the inverse of David's.

Once the narrative is released from the voice of the primary narrator (into a third-person 'shared' voice) the Gardens emerge as having a doubled chronotopic identity, reminding us strongly that spatial experience is determined by perspective and narrative voice (Bakhtin's 'horizon'). In the account of Kensington Gardens *by day* the chronotopes were determined by the adult narrator and thus dominated by 'road' and 'encounter' as he and his ward circled the grounds. By contrast in the sub-narrative for Peter (told in the third person and supposedly co-created by adult and child) the same places *at night* become 'castles'. Peter is in the wrong place at the wrong time to such an extent that he upsets the order of things:

> Peter heard the little people crying everywhere that there was a human in the Gardens after Lock-out Time, but he never thought for a moment that he was the human.... Every living thing was shunning him. (Barrie, [1906] 1991: 15)

In terms of being inside when he should be out, Peter is the child in danger (notably he is not *himself* a figure of danger, as he will later become). Of course this in turn changes for Peter once he finds his nest and the night-time Gardens become his home. *Now* the park at night is a 'castle' to all other children, but an 'idyll' to him. At the same time, though, Peter stands for non-conformity and imaginative freedom from the potentially repressive effects of the adults. The description of him as a 'Betwixt and Between' refers ostensibly to his identity (half-human) but also strongly to his spatiality. The adult voice tries to control the child, but Peter's narrative resists and escapes.

When we compare the Topoi map for *Peter Pan in Kensington Gardens* with the Deep Chronotope map (both maps from the same series generated from the same coded text), then the latter confirms this reading of an emerging tension between adult and child in relation to the place and space of the Gardens (see Figure 33). Here, purple lines represent direct movement in the world. The narrator takes a turn around the social space of the park, registered in the chronotope of the 'public square' but also with 'castle' figuring strongly. The mesh topology shows real/adult and imagined/child spatialities to be tightly interconnected (another kind of nest) but with a sense of the imaginary space (in orange, dominated by the chronotope of the idyll) pulling away from the real – as if one space is trying to free itself from the other.

When we look back to Rackham's map for the first edition, we can see that the river flows off the right-hand side of the image so that Peter's island is left

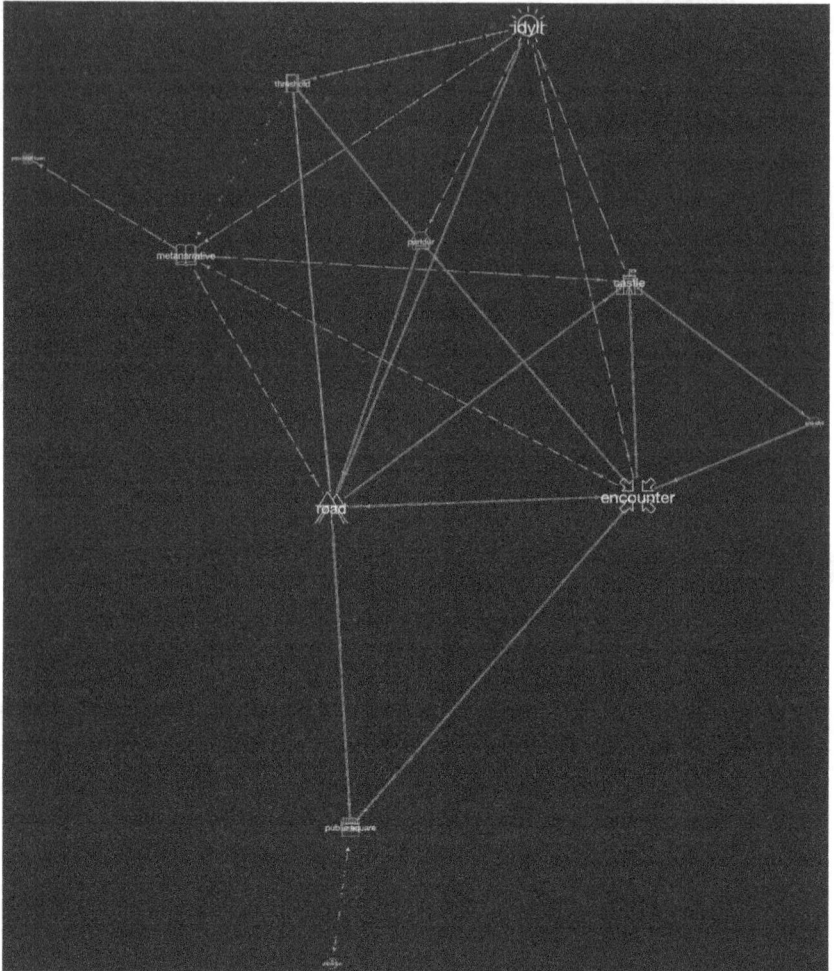

Figure 33 Deep Chronotope map for *Peter Pan in Kensington Gardens*.

hanging in suspended (non-representational) space beyond the frame. If we return from this to the text we find that an indeterminate space is explicitly registered within it along with the first mention of Peter:

> A small part only of the Serpentine is in the Gardens, for soon it passes beneath a bridge to far away where the island is on which all the birds are born that become baby boys and girls. No one who is human, except Peter Pan (and he is only half human), can land on the island. (Barrie, [1906] 1991: 9–10)

Here the mention of 'to far away', almost in passing, is perhaps the first gesturing towards Never Land. The island in the Serpentine as Peter's place of origin, escape, and refuge is both deeply nested within the park but also threatens to break off into another kind of time-space – as it will do in the next version of the text.

```
<topos type = "castle" framename = "the Baby Walk">
At first he found some difficulty in balancing himself on a branch, but presently he remembered the way, and fell asleep. He awoke long before morning, shivering, and saying to himself, 'I never was out on such a cold night'; he had really been out on colder nights when he was a bird, but, of course, as everybody knows, what seems a warm night to a bird is a cold night to a boy in a nightgown. Peter also felt strangely uncomfortable, as if his head was stuffy; he heard loud noises that made him look round sharply, though they were really himself sneezing. There was something he wanted very much, but, though he knew he wanted it, he could not think what it was. What he wanted so much was his mother to blow his nose, but that never struck him, so he decided to appeal to the fairies for enlightenment. They are reputed to know a good deal. </topos>

<topos type = "castle" framename = "Kensington Gardens">
Despairing of the fairies, he resolved to consult the birds, but now he remembered, as an odd thing, that all the birds on the weeping-beech had flown away when he alighted on it, and though this had not troubled him at the time, he saw its meaning now. Every living thing was shunning him. Poor little Peter Pan! he sat down and cried, and even then he did not know that, for a bird, he was sitting on his wrong part. It is a blessing that he did not know, for otherwise he would have lost faith in his power to fly, and the moment you doubt whether you can fly, you cease for ever to be able to do it. The reason birds can fly and we can't is simply that they have perfect faith, for to have faith is to have wings.
```

Figure 34 Marked up text for *Peter Pan in Kensington Gardens*.

Reading the Totality: Detaching Neverland

A comparative mapping model can work in a number of ways: to compare absolute and relative mapping (as in Section 2); in terms of different forms of cartographic representation; to compare chronotopic maps from a series generated from a single text (with different elements of spatial meaning prioritised through the visualisation); or to compare the same map form across different texts. We want now to consider the changing nature of represented space across different textual forms and the corresponding maps.

When we look at Barrie's 1903–04 playscript as part of a textual and spatial process, we can see that it represents a weird amalgam of what comes before and after it. It is sandwiched between the two earliest versions of *Peter Pan*: the sub-narrative held within *The Little White Bird* in 1901, and the publication of this independently as *Peter Pan in Kensington Gardens* in 1906. The first narrative setting of Kensington Gardens is transposed onto the second of the play, where many elements are retained (the little house; Peter Pan's boat with sails) but it is simply enlarged. In the second textual version, Peter is situated in both worlds – released into his own alternative universe but also in the end anchored back to the original Peter of the Gardens (since he returns and lives with Wendy in her house here).

In this first version of the play, Barrie begins to enlarge and separate out his spheres of realist London/safe adult world and Peter's free (but unsafe) world of imaginative child's play. These are no longer nested as they previously were. Spatially, a linkage between the two texts is provided by the presence of the Serpentine within Kensington Gardens and its enlargement into the 'Pirate River' in scene II of the play: '*The scene is a mysterious Forest with a river running through it*' (Barrie, [1903–04] 2019: 77). Neverland is named, but not fully developed. There is no direct telling or showing of the children travelling to it: Wendy simply describes Peter as wanting to 'take us far away over the sea' (Barrie, [1903–04] 2019: 76). Again, after Rose, we can see how narrative voice itself has a spatial dimension, but now the adult narrator's desire for control is rendered invisible and marginal (in the stage directions), while represented adult and child spaces are sundered.

Equally, (and perhaps surprisingly) in the first play, there is no sense of Neverland as an *island*. Instead the shift of form into drama results in a very localised setting for each scene. There is a lack of named places beyond the immediate and a tight focus on small-scale localised environments or sites within those: the home underground, the ship, the bed, and so on. The final scene of the 1903–04 play (entirely removed from later versions of play and prose) attempts to anchor it *back* within Kensington Gardens – as if Neverland has only ever been a kind of dream of escape, or the imagination. Not only is Peter himself recuperated – brought back to live with Wendy in her little house in the park – but so too are all the other characters, with Hook given an alternative identity: '*dressed as schoolmaster in cap and gown and carrying birch*' (Barrie, [1903–04] 2019: 133). His prime motive remains the same but is now given a real-world justification:

> HOOK: That's Wendy, and she has broken the law by not sending her boy to school. Come, bully, let's catch them – Peter *I'll* look after, and Mother Wendy, she shall go to jail! They can't escape me, I have assistant masters watching at all the gates. (Barrie, [1903–04] 2019: 134)

Above all, in this final scene there is no sense in which Peter will return to Neverland. Instead the characters have been relocated and domesticated. This also emphasises the way in which Peter and Neverland are not identical at this point, as they later become.

The Topoi maps, compared across the four core texts, are quite dramatically distinctive (see Figures 35–38), showing both the changing nature of the whole, of adult–child dynamics, and the effects of literary form upon the representation of place and space. In the maps of the two earliest texts there is a strong anchor at the heart of both – 'Kensington Gardens' and 'The Nursery' – as safe, adult-controlled environments. By comparison the maps for the two later texts present far more oppositional spatial forms. Instead of one space being safely contained within another, the two worlds of adult and child (control and freedom; realism and imagination) are set increasingly against each other. By the final 1928 play version, the links between them only occur materially through the metatextual stage directions (shown faintly in green). So a relatively non-threatening space increasingly evolves into something far more disturbing that sets the adult world *against* that of the child.

The most distinctive map is that for the first play version (Figure 36). Here 'The Nursery' functions as a hub, a knot that draws tight the topological ring that represents the leap into the imaginative space of Neverland, but also loops safely home to be resolved in the real-world place of the Gardens. (Of course, from another point of view this looks more like a noose.) It is worth noting that the text for the early version of the play (second map) was marked up by a different coder (SCB) than for the other three texts (RH). So it may be that the subjectivity of the coder also bears upon the distinctiveness of the visualisation for the 1903–04 play. In this sense, the maps generated possess a kind of visual style (as considered at the end of Section 1).

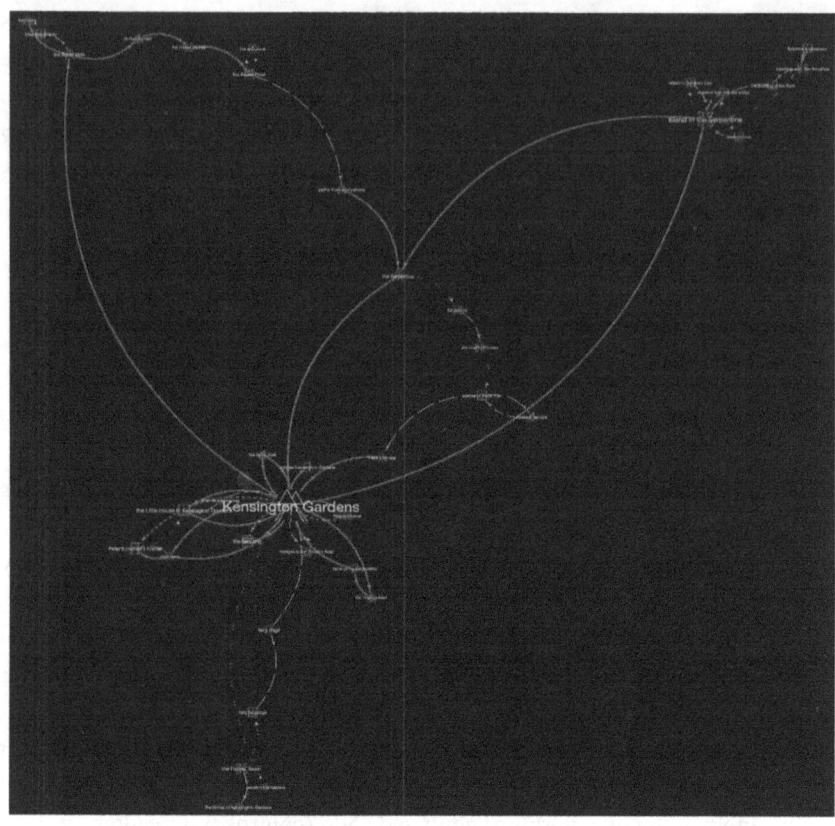

Figure 35 Topoi map for *Peter Pan in Kensington Gardens*.

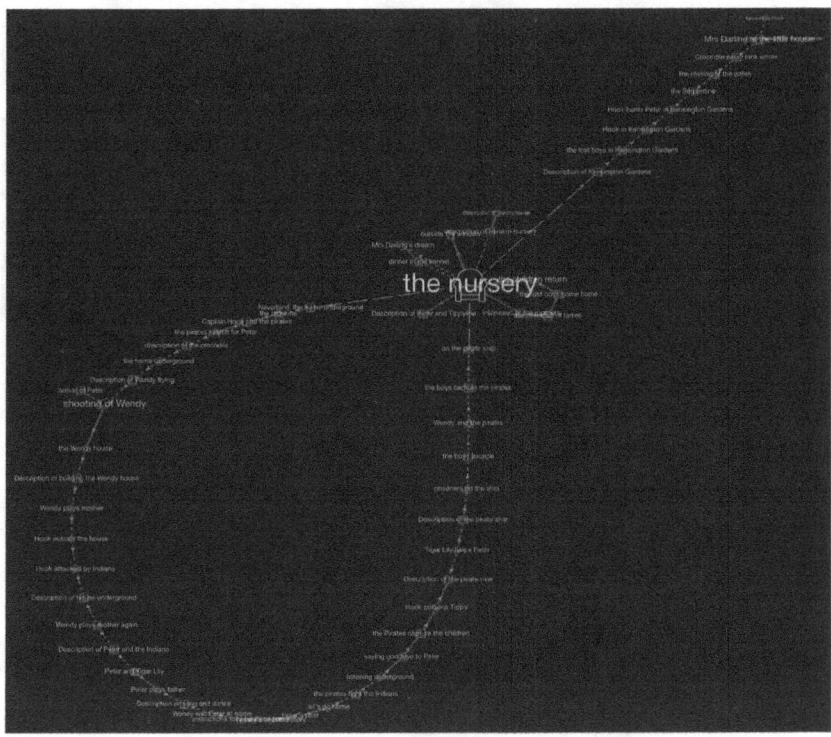

Figure 36 Topoi map for 1902–03 play version.

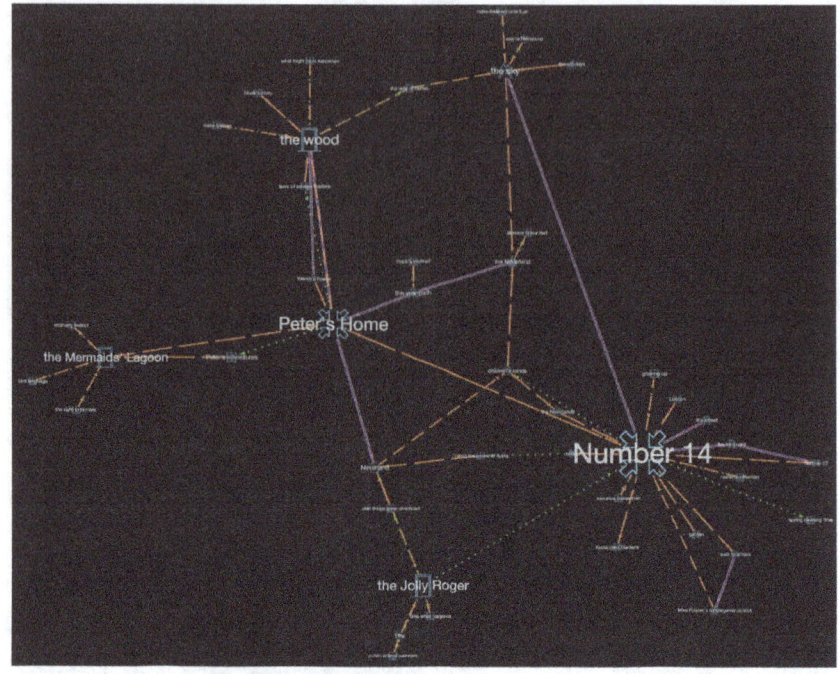

Figure 37 Topoi map for *Peter Pan and Wendy*.

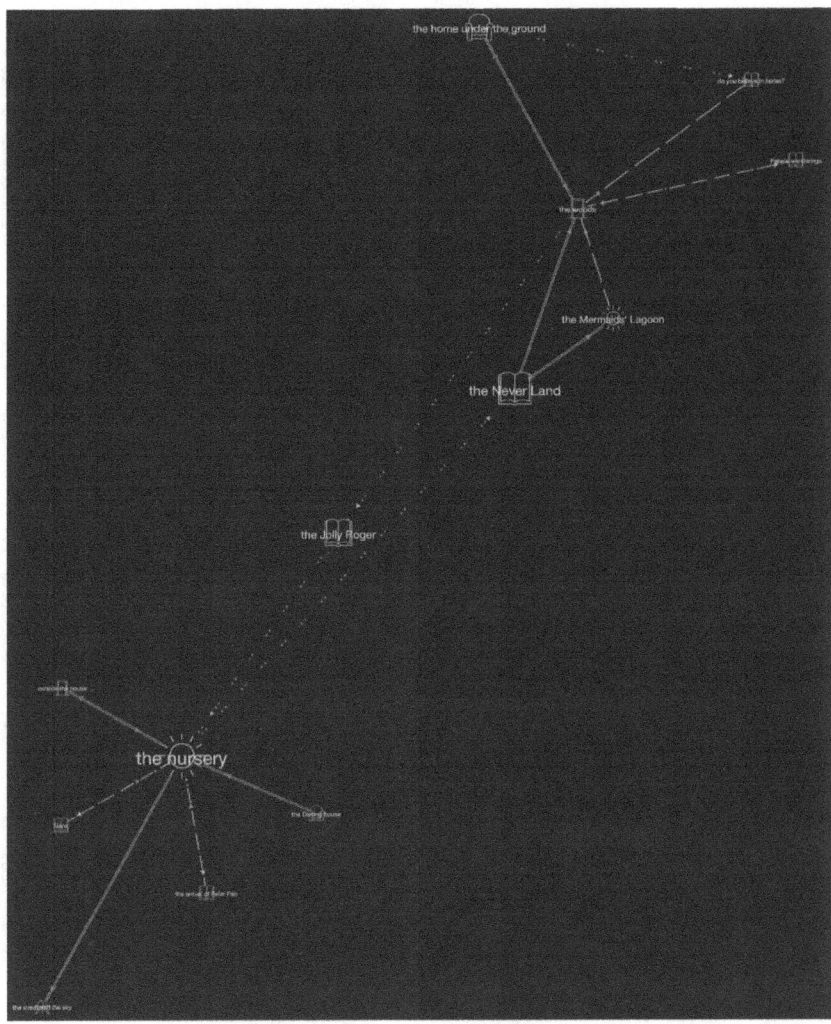

Figure 38 Topoi map for 1928 play version.

We can undertake the same comparative exercise for the Deep Chronotope map (Figures 39–42) which shows the proportion of text given to each underlying spatio-temporal type and movement between such spaces. Here the maps, again, show great variation but this is centred upon the changing relationship between direct experience of realist locations (purple) and indirect or imaginary space (orange). For *Peter Pan in Kensington Gardens*, as already noted, the dominant chronotopes are those of 'encounter' and 'road' but also with 'castle' figuring strongly for Peter. For the 1903–04 play,

86   *Digital Literary Studies*

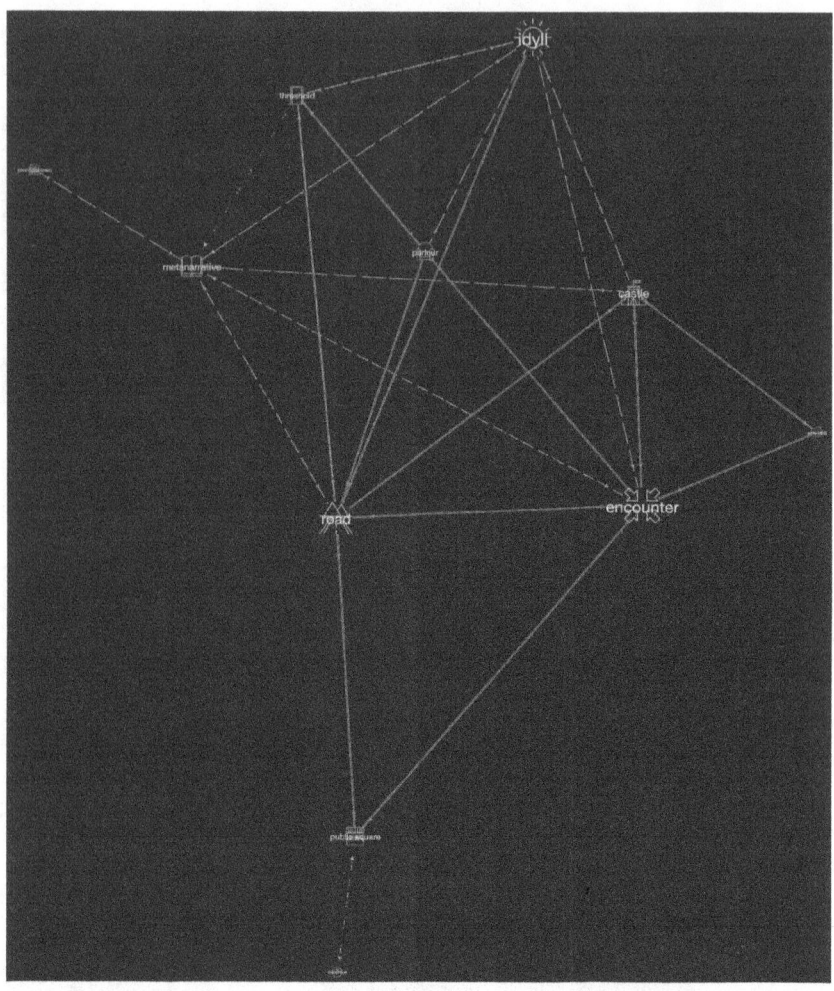

Figure 39 Deep Chronotope map for *Peter Pan in Kensington Gardens*.

New Approaches for Digital Literary Mapping 87

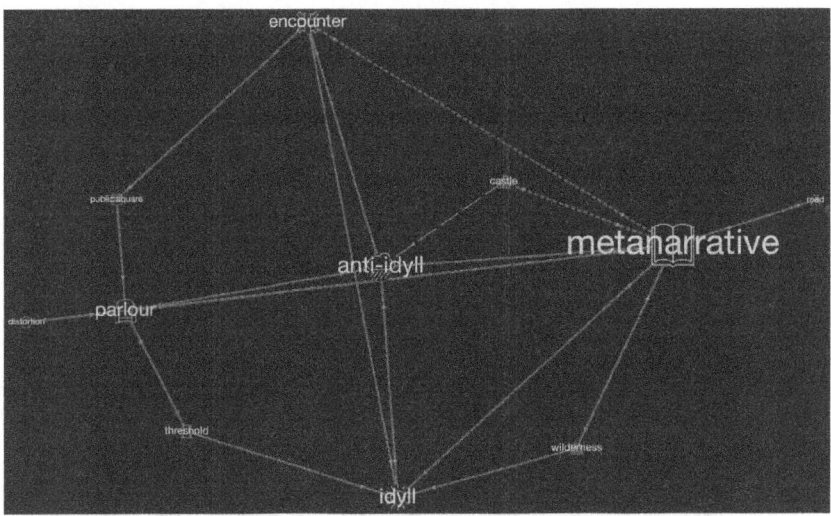

Figure 40 Deep Chronotope map for 1902–03 play version.

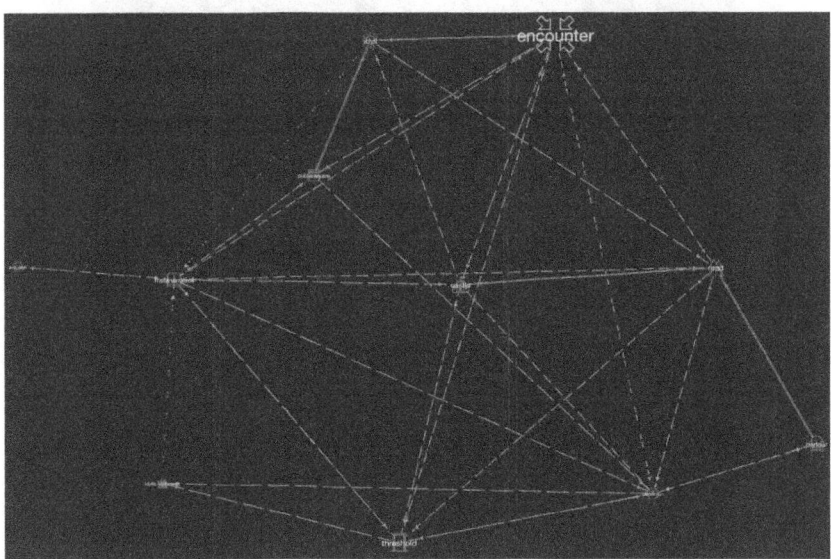

Figure 41 Deep Chronotope map for *Peter Pan and Wendy*.

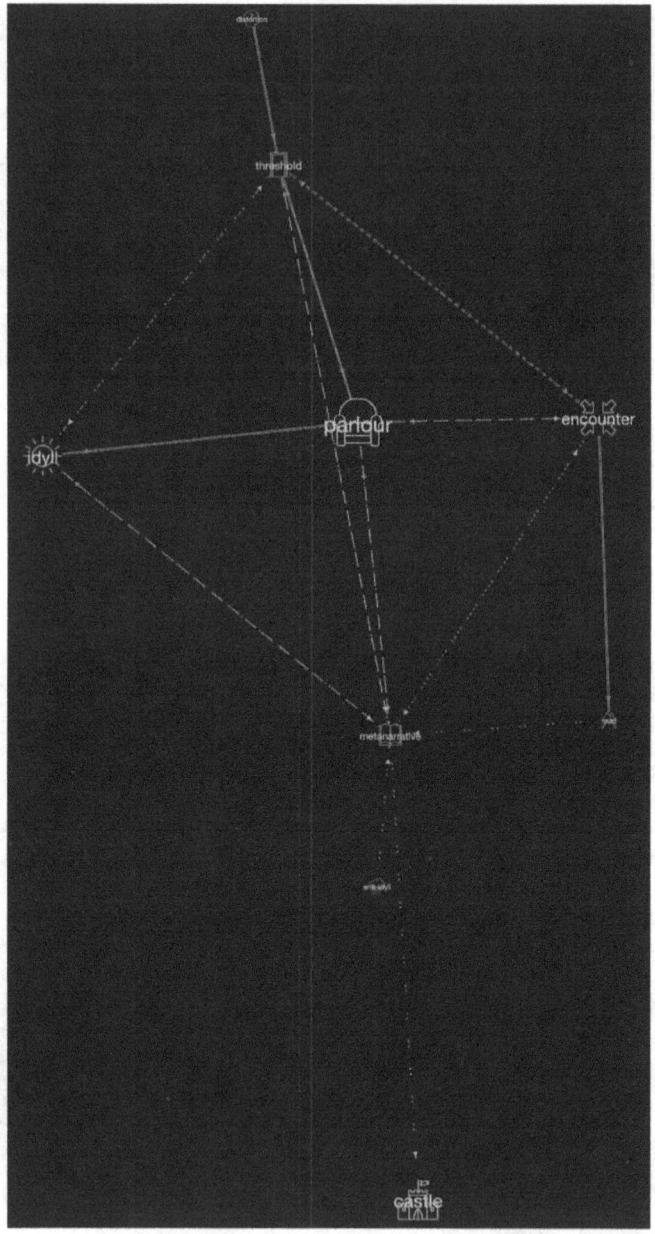

Figure 42 Deep Chronotope map for 1928 play version.

metanarrative emerges strongly as a result of the change of genre and the shift of the controlling adult voice into the textual space of the stage directions. Equally clear though is the emergence of 'anti-idyll' as the central point of a cross. The map is strongly purple, signalling a sense of grounded rather than imaginary locations with direct movement between them (the localised nature of each act in the first play creates this) and Neverland is not fully articulated.

In contrast, the next map for *Peter and Wendy* is dominated by orange, signalling numerous jumps between chronotopes and the dominance of the spatial imaginary. This partly reflects a shift of literary form – as narrative voice relocates again from metatextual stage directions into that of a third person narrator who repeatedly intervenes and comments on the base narrative. It also illustrates the greater significance given to the larger imaginative space of Neverland as it is fully developed. In fact, just as Peter himself emerged as an alter ego for David (out of the shared creative space of adult and child), so Neverland is an amalgam of the other children's imaginative play, but one that threatens to lose its anchor.

The increasing separation of realist/adult and imaginative/child spaces comes to a climax in the map of the 1928 play which generates a rare kite topology. A kite form is a quadrilateral whose four sides can be grouped into two pairs of equal and adjacent sides. In terms of literary topology, it suggests a text in which chronotopic locations are balanced or even mirror each other. This is a product of a dualistic spatial identity within a text. In the case of *Peter Pan*, the spatial tension between adult and child desires is here pushed to its extreme as the play space strongly juxtaposes the safety of the London nursery with the excitement and danger of an unvisitable island beyond the reach of adults. However, where in the first text the adult provided the 'tour', now Peter is both map *and* guide. He transports the children to a place that only seems to truly come into being when he arrives: 'The whole island, in short, which has been having a slack time in Peter's absence, is now in a ferment because the tidings has leaked out that he is on his way back' (Barrie, [1928] 2019: 357). At the same time there is also a layering of spaces as the real is in danger of being supplanted by the fictional. The 'parlour' chronotope at the centre of the map visualisation corresponds to 'the home underground' on the island which itself overlays the real space of 'the nursery' (also corresponding to this chronotope). Thus, the 'I'll be mother' play of Wendy spatially threatens to displace the real world altogether. The map makes explicit a deep anxiety and concern within the text as play threatens to supplant the true order of things and the younger children rapidly forget who their actual parents are and the world they have left behind: 'Wendy (with misgivings): "perhaps we don't remember the old life as well as we thought we did"' (Barrie, [1928] 2019: 405).

Neverland as Chronotope

The very name of the island is unstable:

Never Never Never Land	(1903–04 play)
Neverland	(*Peter and Wendy*)
Never Never Land	(1928 play)

In the late nineteenth century, 'The Never Never Land' was a term used for the Australian Outback in the Northern Territories.[34] It suggested the remotest possible region, a place to which one would definitely *not* want to go. Applied to Peter's island it is less clear whether Neverland is negative or positive. Is it 'the Never Land' because adults can never return to it (a nostalgic lost place), because one cannot get there at all without Peter (unattainable), or a place of childhood imaginative escape that somehow becomes real (it should never exist)? Or is it still, as it always was, a place one should not desire to visit at all?

Chronotopically speaking, what is the identity of Neverland? It is a famous literary island, although, as we have seen, not until the third version of the text. It is a kind of Utopian/Dystopian space (the rare 'kite' form for the deep map of the 1928 play compares with that generated out of the text of Thomas More's *Utopia* shown in Figure 43). It is held in suspended space and time. It is also a representation within a representation; a projection from one space to another; a shared space, composite. It is a paradox, a cognitive map that can be seen, the inner world made the outer. In *Peter and Wendy*, a full and contradictory account is given:

> I don't know whether you have ever seen a map of a person's mind. Doctors sometimes draw maps of other parts of you, and your own map can become intensely interesting, but catch them trying to draw a map of a child's mind, which is not only confused, but keeps going round all the time. There are zigzag lines on it, just like your temperature on a card, and these are probably roads in the island; for the Neverland is always more or less an island, with astonishing splashes of colour here and there, and coral reefs and rakish-looking craft in the offing, and savages and lonely lairs, and gnomes who are mostly tailors, and caves through which a river runs, and princes with six elder brothers, and a hut fast

---

[34] Douglas-Fairhurst refers to adventure and travel books of the time using this term: A. W. Stirling, *The Never Never Land: A Ride in North Queensland* (1884) and Wilson Barrett, *The Never-Never Land* (1902).

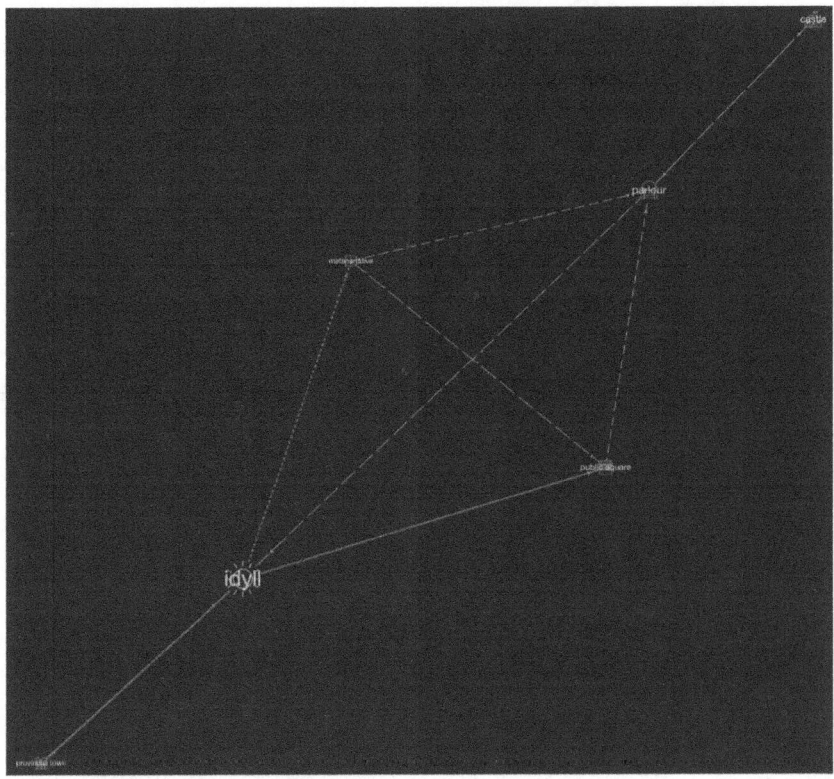

Figure 43 Deep Chronotope map for Utopia.

Table 6 Bakhtinian chronotopes and genre in *Peter Pan*

Macro-genre	Unifying chronotopic identity	Nature of hero	Emerging genres	Sub-chronotopic motifs
Fantasy/Nightmare	Flux, inversion, ability for one space to become another	Unreliable, of the moment, out of time	Children's fiction utopia/dystopia	Encounter, road, castle, idyll, anti-idyll

going to decay, and one very small old lady with a hooked nose. It would be an easy map if that were all; but there is also first day at school, religion, fathers, the Round Pond, needlework, murders, hangings, verbs that take the dative, chocolate-pudding day, getting into braces, say ninety-nine, threepence for pulling out your tooth yourself, and so on; and either these are part of the island or they are another map showing through, and it is all rather confusing, especially as nothing will stand still. (Barrie, [1911] 2019: 146–47)

This, then, is a highly contradictory space, one that morphs between actual locations and moments of real life, the dreamed, the read, the imagined, and one that resists all attempts to map it either by adult or child. In the mark-up for this passage the text is coded as a 'distortion' but in comparison with the text itself this only really serves to make clear the limits of our chronotopic model since so much more is going on in terms of the intermingling of adult and child voice and perspective than this tag can allow for.

If we think back to the table of Bakhtin's macro-genres discussed in Section 2, we might produce for *Peter Pan* something that looks like Table 6. Above all, it is clear that what Neverland 'is' to one person is very different from what it is to another. The nature of the experience it provides depends on the person who enters it and even then it is worryingly changeable. What to the children is a fantastic adventure, to their parents is a traumatic abduction, but one identity constantly threatens to become another. It is self-consciously both immaterial and material. It is the ultimate literary space threatening to exceed the imagination that projects it and the language that describes it. Its master identity as a chronotope can only be defined paradoxically in terms of having *no* fixed identity, of being constantly in flux. This identity ripples outward from it – applying also both to Peter as hero/anti-hero and to the text itself, destabilising everything. Chronotopic mapping has the potential to visualise this in ways not able to be explored here – for example through a series of sub-maps for different key locations (park, nursery, and island) across texts, or in terms of emotional valence in relation to different characters – but still the text resists all attempts at visual representation.

Neverland doesn't simply reverse the power dynamic (the children make the map, create the space of their dreams, and imagination is released); its evolution across forms emphasises negation of the safe space. It is threatening to the adult, but it is also ultimately threatening to the child. Again, like Peter, it turns spaces inside out. Instead of being safely contained – the 'map of a child's mind' (that cannot be externalised) – the imaginary now threatens to entirely displace the everyday: 'Thus sharply did the terrified three learn the difference between an island of make-believe and the same island come true' (Barrie, [1911] 2019: 178). It is worth noting that the narrator at this point in the text, where Neverland is most threatening, reverts to the use of second person that so dominated *Peter Pan in Kensington Gardens*:[35]

> In the old days at home the Neverland had always begun to look a little dark and threatening by bedtime. Then unexplored patches arose in it and spread; black shadows moved about in them; the roar of the beasts of prey was quite different now, and above all, you lost the certainty that you would win. You were quite glad that the night-lights were in. You even liked Nana to say that this was just the mantelpiece over here, and that the Neverland was all make-believe.
>
> Of course the Neverland had been make-believe in those days; but it was real now, and there were no night-lights, and it was getting darker every moment, and where was Nana? (Barrie, [1911] 2019: 175)

The day/night duality of the park (the threat of Lock-out time) is replayed onto Neverland. Dusk is the time that it threatens to exceed itself: 'In the daytime you think the Never Land is only make-believe, and so it is to the likes of you, but this is the Never Land come true' (Barrie, [1928] 2019: 358). At issue here is the question of who controls and generates the spatio-temporal and whether it proceeds from the child (who can then choose to withdraw from it) or whether it encompasses and threatens to entrap him or her. Neverland seems almost to acquire agency of its own. As all adult ability to control or protect the children is lost, place itself becomes predatory:

---

[35] Note Rose's point that: 'The issue of narrative position in language takes on the physical quality of location or place' (Rose, 1984: 72). This is certainly true in relation to spatial affect.

> [T]hey drew near the Neverland; for after many moons they did reach it, and, what is more, they had been going pretty straight all the time, not perhaps so much owing to the guidance of Peter or Tink as because the island was out looking for them. (Barrie, [1911] 2019: 173)

Play is only definable as play *because it ends*: the park gates close at the end of the day. A place of permanent play is an impossible paradox and not pleasurable at all. Ultimately, such a space is disturbing to *both* adults and children precisely *because* it is an exact inversion of the safe and contained area of the park, with its bounds of space and time, from which it emerged originally. There is a sense in which Peter's world is *neither* that of the adult nor that of the child, as this spatial tug of war suggests, but increasingly somewhere that nobody really wants to inhabit permanently (not even Peter).

Reading the texts through the maps, and the maps through the text, draws out the shifting adult–child dynamics and corresponding spatial tensions across the totality extremely clearly. An iterative model of interpretation connects the readings of map–text–reader–character in a complex, unstable, and shifting interplay. At the same time, because the maps are themselves multiple and iterative, they are able to partly pull against a teleological reading of the texts and allow us to respond to the whole as one of continually moving and reshaping parts. A visual/verbal analysis thus releases us into a greater range of formal juxtapositions that run right across: map versus tour, margin versus centre, inner versus outer, contained versus free, safe versus endangered, and adult versus child. The instability of text, person, and place generates a multiplicity of spatial forms that are themselves bound up with the complexity of tensions between adult and child spaces over time. At the same time the complexity of the *Peter Pan* totality constantly reminds us of the power of literary place and space to not only exceed but also entirely disrupt our conventional spatial understanding.

4 Conclusion

We hope that this brief Element has both engaged with some of the core concerns of digital literary mapping and put forward a convincing new approach (the iterative visual/verbal method) that is more closely aligned to traditional critical analysis and interpretation than other DH approaches and deeply embedded in the core meanings of the text. Again, we want to stress that we see no need for one single kind of reading or mapping to dominate, and our experience has led us to believe that a comparative mapping method is the most illuminating. Thus we advocate the bringing together of automated and manual, quantitative and qualitative, GIS/geovisual, and more Humanities-centred 2D and 3D visualisation tools in hybrid projects, going forward.

Even in the comparative and combined approach that we advocate here, there is room for critique. For example, Bruno Latour argues *against* nesting as 'a confusion of scale, [that] runs the risk of making leaps of cognition or oversimplifying causality' (Springett, 2015: 629). In his discussion of maps and narratives in 'Anti-zoom', Latour treats the concept of zoom as an illusion, arguing that one should not confuse 'projection with connectivity' (Latour, 2014: 99) and that the relationship between connections is 'not hierarchical but heterarchical' (97). This opens up digital mapping by means of graph topology even further, posing questions about what, why, and how we map. Perhaps literary mapping should not be concerned with the dominance of narrative structure, plot dynamics or character movement across a landscape but with other less immediately obvious elements such as causality and agency (human and non-human) which are also of fundamental importance to literary meaning and, indeed, the human condition.

Chronotopic Cartography is really only a starting point in terms of enriching the field and allowing for a plurality of DH methods for Literary Studies. There is still much to do here. The tools and user interface could be made far more accessible – and this is another key area of DH requiring development for the Humanities. Our multiple map layers are crude and one can envisage a far more sophisticated future model – a kind of 'time cube' with multiple layers of maps that could be slid in and out (rather like the pleasing interface for re-ordering layers of images on a Mac) but also viewed as a totality. Then sub-mapped elements such as different characters' movements, narrative voice, key events, and so on could be viewed discretely (each individual layer) or as a totality seen from above.

Our model incorporates time by using the combined form of the chronotope, but there remains a strong tendency for the 2D maps to privilege the spatial over the temporal. A 3D dynamic model (thus actually 4D) could respect the full complexity of time for literature: the unfolding temporality of reading, the extent of the text itself, and of evolving spatio-temporal meanings and tensions across it. Equally, once we release the act of mapping from the need for it to be anchored in real-world geography and make the relative maps dynamic, this allows the possibility of mapping more intangible elements of literary spatiality that change over time: power dynamics, emotional affect, and causality. Such approaches have great future potential, not just for Literary Studies but also for closely related disciplines such as History or Religious Studies, Gender Studies, Post-Colonialism, and beyond.

References

Bailey, J. & Biggs, I. (2012). 'Either Side of Delphy Bridge': A Deep Mapping Project Evoking and Engaging the Lives of Older Adults in Rural North Cornwall. *Journal of Rural Studies* 28, 318–28.

Bakhtin, M. M. [1924] (1990). The Problem of Content, Material and Form in Verbal Art. In M. Holquist & V. Liapunov, eds., *Art and Answerability: Early Philosophical Essays by M. M. Bakhtin*. Austin: University of Texas Press, 261–62.

[1936–8] (1986). The *Bildungsroman* and Its Significance in the History of Realism (Towards a Historical Typography of the Novel). In V. W. McGee, trans., C. Emerson & M. Holquist, eds., *Speech Genres and Other Late Essays*. Austin: University of Texas Press, 10–59.

[1937] (1984). Forms of Time and of the Chronotope in the Novel. In M. Holquist, ed., *The Dialogic Imagination*, Austin: University of Texas Press, 84–258.

[1963] (1984). *Problems of Dostoevsky's Poetics*. C. Emerson, ed., Minneapolis: University of Minneapolis Press.

[1974] (1986). Towards a Methodology for the Human Sciences. In C. Emerson & M. Holquist, eds., *Speech Genres and Other Late Essays*. Austin: University of Texas Press, 159–72.

Bakhtin, M. M. & Medvedev, P. N. (1978). *The Formal Method in Literary Scholarship*. A. J. Wehrle, trans., Baltimore: Johns Hopkins Press.

Barrie, J. M. [1903–04] (2019). Anon: A Play. In R. D. Fairhurst, ed., *The Collected Peter Pan*. Oxford: Oxford University Press, 53–140.

[1906] (1991). Peter Pan in Kensington Gardens. In P. Hollindale, ed., *Peter Pan in Kensington Gardens and Peter and Wendy*. Oxford: Oxford University Press, 1–65.

[1911] (2019). Peter and Wendy. In R. D. Fairhurst, ed., *The Collected Peter Pan*, Oxford: Oxford University Press, 141–276.

[1928] (2019). Peter Pan, or the Boy Who Would Not Grow Up. In R. D. Fairhurst, ed., *The Collected Peter Pan*. Oxford: Oxford University Press, 321–410.

Beames, T. (1852). *The Rookeries of London*. London: Thomas Bosworth.

Bemong, N., Borghart, P., & De Dobbeleer, M. (2010). Bakhtin's Theory of the Literary Chronotope: Reflections, Applications, Perspectives. Kristoffel Demoen et al., ed., Gent, Belgium: Academia Press.

Bodenhamer, D., Corrigan, J. & Harris, T. (2013). Deep Mapping and the Spatial Humanities. *International Journal of Humanities and Arts Computer* 7 (1), 170–75.

Bodenhamer, D. J., Corrigan, J. & Harris, T. (2017). Introduction. In D. J. Bodenhamer, J. Corrigan & T. Harris, eds. *Deep Maps and Spatial Narratives*. Bloomington and Indianapolis: Indiana University Press, 1–6.

Brown, P. (2006). Introduction. In P. Brown & M. Irwin, eds., *Literature and Place, 1800–2000*. Bern: Peter Lang, 13–24.

Budgen, F. (1972). *James Joyce and the Making of 'Ulysses'*. Oxford: Oxford University Press.

Bushell, S. (2016). Mapping Fiction: Spatialising the Literary Work. In D. Cooper, C. Donaldson & P. Murrieta-Flores, eds., *Literary Mapping in the Digital Age*. London: Routledge, 125–46.

   (2020). *Reading and Mapping Fiction: Spatialising the Literary Text*. Cambridge: Cambridge University Press.

Bushell, S., Butler, J., Hay, D. & Hutcheon, R. (2022a). 'Digital Literary Mapping I: Visualising and Reading Graph Topologies as Maps for Literature'. *Cartographica*, 57(1), 11–36.

Bushell, S., Butler, J., Hay, D. & Hutcheon, R. (2022b). 'Digital Literary Mapping II: Towards an Integrated Visual-Verbal Method for the Humanities'. *Cartographica*, 57(1), 37–64.

Buzard, J. (2005). *Disorienting Fiction: The Autoethnographic Work of Nineteenth-Century British Novels*. Princeton: Princeton University Press.

Charles Booth's London: Poverty Maps and Police Notebooks (2016). London: Thames & Hudson. https://booth.lse.ac.uk.

Cole, T. & Hahmann, T. (2019). Geographies of the Holocaust: Experiments in GIS, QSR and Graph Representations. *International Journal of Humanities and Arts Computing* 13 (1–2), 39–52.

Cooper, D. & Gregory, I. (2011). Mapping the English Lake District: A Literary GIS. *Transactions of Human Geography* 36 (1), 89–108.

Cooper, D., & Priestnall, G. (2011). The Processual Intertextuality of Literary Cartographies: Critical and Digital Practices. *The Cartographic Journal*, 48(4), 250–262.

De Certeau, M. [1980] (1984). *The Practice of Everyday Life*, S. Randall, trans. Berkeley: University of California Press.

Dickens, C. [1838] (1966). *Oliver Twist*. K. Tillotson, ed., Oxford: Oxford University Press.

Dickens, C. [1837–8] (2003). *Oliver Twist*. Philip Horne, ed., Harmondsworth: Penguin.

Douglas-Fairhurst, R., ed. (2019). *The Collected Peter Pan*. Oxford: Oxford University Press.

Drucker, J. (2012). Humanistic Theory and Digital Scholarship. In M. K. Gold, ed., *Debates in the Digital Humanities*. Minneapolis: University of Minnesota Press, 85–95.

  (2014). *Graphesis: Visual Forms of Knowledge Production*. Cambridge, MA: Harvard University Press.

Earl, R. (2019). *Topology: A Very Short Introduction*. Oxford: Oxford University Press.

Elson, D. K., Dames, N. & McKeown, K. (2010). Extracting Social Networks from Literary Fiction. Proceedings of the 48th Annual Meeting of the Association for Computational Linguistics. Uppsala Sweden, 138–47.

English, J. F. & Underwood, T. (2016). Shifting Scales: Between Literature and Social Science. *Modern Language Quarterly* 77 (3), 277–95.

Eve, M. P. (2019). *Close Reading with Computers: Textual Scholarship, Computational Formalism and David Mitchell's Cloud Atlas*, Stanford: Stanford University Press.

  (2022). *The Digital Humanities and Literary Studies*, Oxford: Oxford University Press.

Fishkin, S. F. (2011). Deep Maps: A Brief for Digital Palimpsestic Mapping Projects. *Journal of Transactional American Studies* 3 (2). https://escholarship.org/uc/item/92v100t0.

Foucault, M. [1967] (1986). Of Other Spaces. Originally Des Espace Autres. J. Miskoweic, trans. *Diacritics* 16 (1), 22–27.

Friedman, S. (1993). Spatialisation: A Strategy for Reading Narrative. Narrative 1 (1), 12–23.

  (2008). Spatial Poetics and Arundhati Roy's The God of Small Things. In J. Phelan & P. J. Rabinowitz, eds., A Companion to Narrative Theory. Oxford: Blackwell, 192–205.

Harley, J. B. (1989). Deconstructing the Map. *Cartographica* 26(2), 1–20.

Harvey, D. (1989). *The Condition of Postmodernity*. New York: Blackwell.

  (1996). *Justice, Nature and the Geography of Difference*, Malden: Blackwell.

Heuser, R., Moretti, F. & Steiner. E. (2016). LiteraryLabPamphlet13, The Emotions of London. https://litlab.stanford.edu/LiteraryLabPamphlet13.pdf.

Hillis Miller, J. (1995). *Topographies*. Stanford: Stanford University Press.

Hollindale, P., ed. (1991). *Peter Pan in Kensington Gardens and Peter and Wendy*. Oxford: Oxford University Press.

Holquist, M. (1990). *Dialogism: Bakhtin and His World*, New York: Routledge.

Housman, A. E. [1896] (2010). *A Shropshire Lad and Other Poems*. A. Burnett, ed., London: Penguin Books.

Jack, R. D. S. (1990). The Manuscript of *Peter Pan*. *Children's Literature*, 18, 101–113.

Jameson, F. (1990). *Postmodernism, or the Cultural Logic of Late Capitalism*. Durham: Duke University Press.

Jin, J. (2017). Problems of Scale in 'Close' and 'Distant' Reading. *Philological Quarterly*, 96 (1), 105–20.

Jockers, M. L. (2013). *Macroanalysis: Digital Methods and Literary History*. Illinois: University of Illinois.

Joyce, S. (2003). *Capital Offences: Geographies of Class and Crime in Victorian London*. Charlottesville: University of Virginia Press.

Kitchin, R., Dodge, M. & Perkins, C. (2009). Thinking About Maps. In R. Kitchin, M. Dodge & C. Perkins, eds., *Rethinking Maps*, London: Routledge, 1–25.

Kitchin, R., Gleeson, J. & Dodge, M. (2012). Unfolding Mapping Practices: A New Epistemology for Cartography. *Transactions of the Institute of British Geographers* 38 (3), 1–17.

Kitton, Frederick G. (1905). *The Dickens Country*. London: A and C Black.

Lancelyn Green, R. (1954). *Fifty Years of Peter Pan*. London: Peter Davies.

Latour, B. (2014). Anti-zoom. In M. Tavel Clarke & D. Wittenberg, eds., *Scale in Literature and Culture*, Cham: Springer International, 93–101.

Lefebvre, H. (1974). *The Production of Space*. D. Nicholson Smith, trans., Oxford: Blackwells.

Massey, D. (1994). *Space, Place and Gender*. Oxford: Blackwell.

(2005). *For Space*. London: Sage.

McLucas, C. (2013). The Ten Tenets of Deep Mapping. https://cliffordmclucas.info/deep-mapping.html.

Mitchell, P. (2017). Literary Geography and the Digital: The Emergence of Neogeography. In R. Tally, ed., *The Routledge Handbook of Literature and Space*. London, Routledge, 85–94.

Moon, W. L. H. (1991). *PrairyErth: A Deep Map*. Boston: Houghton Mifflin.

Moretti, F. (1998). *Atlas of the European Novel 1800–1900*, London: Verso.

(2005). *Graphs, Maps, Trees*. London: Verso.

(2011). Network Theory, Plot Analysis. Literary Lab: Pamphlet 2. https://litlab.stanford.edu/pamphlets/.

(2013). *Distant Reading*. London: Verso.

Murrieta-Flores, P. & Martins, B. (2019). The Geospatial Humanities: Past, Present and Future. *International Journal of Geographical Information Science* 33 (12), 2424–29.

Piatti, B., Bär, H. R., Reuschel, A.-K., Hurni, L. & Cartwright, W. (2009). Mapping Literature: Towards a Geography of Fiction. In W. Cartwright, G. Gartner & A. Lehn, eds., *Cartography and Art*. Berlin: Springer-Verlag, 177–93.

Piatti, B. & Hurni, L. (2013). Cartographies of Fictional Worlds. *The Cartographic Journal* 48 (4), 218–23.

Piatti. B., Resuchel, A. K. & Hurni, L. (2011). CO237. A Literary Atlas of Europe – Analysing the Geography of Fiction with an Interactive Mapping and Visualisation System. ICC Proceedings. https://icaci.org/files/documents/ICC_proceedings/ICC2011/Oral%20Presentations%20PDF/C2-Map%20in%20narratives%20and%20for%20narratives%20analysis/CO-237.pdf.

Piper, A. (2013). Reading's Refrain: From Bibliography to Topology. *ELH* 80 (2), 373–99.

(2018). *Enumerations: Data and Literary Study.* Chicago: University of Chicago Press.

Pressman, J. & Swanstrom, L. (2013). The Literary and/as the Digital Humanities. *Digital Humanities Quarterly*, 7 (1), 5–12.

Reuschel, A.-K. & Hurni, L. (2011). Mapping Literature: Visualisation of Spatial Uncertainty in Fiction. *The Cartographic Journal*, 48 (4), 293–308.

Reuschel, A.-K, Piatti, B. & Hurni, L. (2009). Mapping Literature: The Prototype of 'A Literary Atlas of Europe'. Proceedings of the 24th International Cartographic Conference, 1–12.

Reuschel, A.-K., Piatti, B. & Hurni, L. (2013). Modelling Uncertain Geodata for the Literary Atlas of Europe. In Kris, K., Cartwright, W. & Kinberger, M. eds., *Understanding Different Geographies, 135 Lecture Notes in Geoinformation and Cartography.* Berlin: Springer-Verlag, 135–157.

Richardson, R. (2015). The Subterranean Topography of Oliver Twist. *Dickens Quarterly* 32 (4), 293–312.

Roberts, L. (2016). Deep Mapping and Spatial Anthropology. *Humanities* 5 (5), 1–7.

Rose, J. (1984). *The Case of Peter Pan or the Impossibility of Children's Fiction.* Philadelphia: University of Pennsylvania Press.

Rydberg-Cox, J. (2011). Social Networks and the Language of Greek Tragedy. *Journal of the Chicago Colloquium on Digital Humanities and Computer Science* 1 (3), 1–11. http://jdhcs.uchicago.edu/.

Shelley, M. [1818] (1996). *Mary Shelley: Frankenstein, the 1818 Text.* J. P. Hunter, ed., New York: W. W. Norton.

Shklovsky, V. [1929] (1990). *Theory of Prose.* B. Sher, trans., London: Dalkey Archive Press.

Soja, E. (1996). *Thirdspace: Journeys to Los Angeles and Other Real-and-Imagined Places.* Oxford: Blackwell.

Springett, S. (2015). Going Deeper or Flatter: Connecting Deep Mapping, Flat Ontologies and the Democratizing of Knowledge. *Humanities* 4 (4), 623–36.

Steiner, P. (2016). *Russian Formalism: A Metapoetics*. Ithaca: Cornell University Press.

Stell, J. (2019). Qualitative Spatial Representation for the Humanities. *International Journal of Humanities and Arts Computing* 123 (1–2), 2–27.

Stirling, K. (2012). *Peter Pan's Shadow in the Literary Imagination*. London: Routledge.

Tally, R. Jr. (2012). *Spatiality*. London: Routledge.

Tambling, J. (2009). *Going Astray: Dickens and London*. Abingdon: Routledge.

Tambling, J. ed. (2012). *Dickens and the City*. Abingdon: Routledge.

Taylor, J. & Gregory, I. (2022). *Deep Mapping the Literary Lake District: A Geographical Text Analysis*. New Jersey: Bucknell University Press.

Taylor, J., Gregory, I. & Donaldson, C. (2018). Combining Close and Distant Reading: A Multiscalar Analysis of the English Lake District's Soundscapes. *International Journal of Humanities and Arts Computing* 12 (2), 163–82.

Taylor, J., Donaldson, C., Gregory, I. & Butler, J. (2018). Mapping Digitally, Mapping Deep: Exploring Digital Literary Geographies. *Literary Geographies* 4 (1), 10–19.

Travis, C. B. (2015). *Abstract Machine: Humanities GIS*. California: Esri Press.
  (2017). Joycean Chronotopography: Homer, Dante, Ulysses. In R. Tally Jr., ed., *The Routledge Handbook of Literature and Space*. London: Routledge, 323–36.

Underwood, T. (2016). Distant Reading and Recent Intellectual History. *Debates in the Digital Humanities* 2016, 530–33. http://dx.doi.org/10.17613/M6288J.

Wolfreys, J. (2012). *Dickens's London: Perception, Subjectivity and Urban Multiplicity*. Edinburgh: Edinburgh University Press.

Acknowledgements

New Approaches for Digital Literary Mapping: Chronotopic Cartography emerges directly from an AHRC funded research project undertaken at Lancaster University from 2017–21. Although this Element is co-authored by Bushell and Hutcheon, it is essential that we fully acknowledge the contributions of the two other members of the core research team: James Butler and Duncan Hay. Without their work on the schema, the underlying models and methods, the development of tools, data visualisations, and web design, the literary-critical interpretations presented here could not have been undertaken. We would also like to thank the Cambridge University Press readers for their sound advice on the first submitted version of this book, which considerably strengthened the presentation of our arguments. The Chronotopic Cartographies project was funded by the Arts and Humanities Research Council in the UK: AH/P00895X/1. The project involved the authors above, with James Butler and Duncan Hay as the core team at Lancaster University, along with the following researchers at Lancaster and other institutions: Dave Beavan, Alex Butterworth, David Cooper, Ian Gregory, James Loxley, Patricia Murrieta-Flores, and Andrew Richardson. We are indebted to these individuals for their generous support.

Digital Literary Studies

Katherine Bode
Australian National University

Katherine Bode is Professor of Literary and Textual Studies at the Australian National University. Her research explores the critical potential and limitations of computational approaches to literature, in publications including *A World of Fiction: Digital Collections and the Future of Literary History* (2018), *Advancing Digital Humanities: Research, Methods, Theories* (2014), *Reading by Numbers: Recalibrating the Literary Field* (2012), and *Resourceful Reading: The New Empiricism, eResearch and Australian Literary Culture* (2009).

Adam Hammond
University of Toronto

Adam Hammond is Assistant Professor of English at the University of Toronto. He is author of *Literature in the Digital Age* (Cambridge 2016) and co-author of *Modernism: Keywords* (2014). He works on modernism, digital narrative, and computational approaches to literary style. He is editor of the forthcoming *Cambridge Companion to Literature in the Digital Age* and *Cambridge Critical Concepts: Literature and Technology*.

Gabriel Hankins
Clemson University

Gabriel Hankins is Associate Professor of English at Clemson University. His first book is *Interwar Modernism and the Liberal World Order* (Cambridge 2019). He writes on modernism, digital humanities, and color. He is technical manager for the Twentieth Century Literary Letters Project and co-editor on *The Digital Futures of Graduate Study in the Humanities* (in progress).

Advisory Board

David Bammen *University of California, Berkeley*
Amy Earhardt *Texas A&M University*
Dirk Van Hulle *University of Oxford*
Fotis Jannidis *Julius-Maximilians-Universität*
Matthew Kirschenbaum *University of Maryland*
Laura Mandell *Texas A&M University*
Élika Ortega-Guzman *University of Colorado, Boulder*
Marisa Parham *Amherst College*
Rita Raley *University of California, Santa Barbara*
Scott Rettberg *University of Bergen*
Roopika Risam *Salem State University*
Glenn Roe *Sorbonne University*
Whitney Trettien *University of Pennsylvania*
Ted Underwood *University of Illinois*

About the Series

Our series provides short exemplary texts that address a pressing research question of clear scholarly interest within a defined area of literary studies, clearly articulate the method used to address the question, and demonstrate the literary insights achieved.

Cambridge Elements

Digital Literary Studies

Elements in the Series

Can We Be wrong? The Problem of Textual Evidence in a Time of Data
Andrew Piper

Literary Geographies in Balzac and Proust
Melanie Conroy

The Shapes of Stories: Sentiment Analysis for Narrative
Katherine Elkins

Actual Fictions: Literary Representation and Character Network Analysis
Roel Smeets

The Challenges of Born-Digital Fiction: Editions, Translations, and Emulations
Dene Grigar and Mariusz Pisarski

New Approaches for Digital Literary Mapping: Chronotopic Cartography
Sally Bushell and Rebecca Hutcheon

A full series listing is available at: www.cambridge.org/EDLS

For EU product safety concerns, contact us at Calle de José Abascal, 56–1°,
28003 Madrid, Spain or eugpsr@cambridge.org.